MEL GEL

Study Guide

Robin Main

ISBN: 0-578-18853-8
ISBN-13: 978-0-578-18853-9

DEDICATION

To all the kings and priests
of the Order of Melchizedek
whose desire is to lead
their inner fire bride forth.

CONTENTS

ACKNOWLEDGMENTS

Special thanks to these wonderful editors:

Tamara Jarvis, Bonnie Klein and Judy Roehl

Thanks to the *Mystic Mentoring (in Christ) Tribe Lead*
for all your love and support:

Karyn Bloom, Rhonda Smathers, Carol Barham, Stephanie Park,
Bonnie Klein, Tamara Jarvis, and Jill Ardemagni.

Give 'em heaven!!!

1 – RESTORATION OF ALL THINGS AND THE ENGRAVINGS

The Order of Melchizedek… The ORDER of Melchizedek… I have had many people get uptight hearing me simply say that people are being made after the Order of Melchizedek. Some seem to think that Jesus Christ, being the High Priest of the Order of Melchizedek, negates the reality of people entering into this Order.

"Melchizedek" is both a name and a title. It's a title for those being made after the Order of Melchizedek. When Scripture states that Yeshua has been *"called of God a high priest after the Order of Melchizedek" (Hebrews 5.10)*, a group of people united in a formal way under the banner of the "Order of Melchizedek" is implied. Groups such as the Order of Saint John may not be familiar to many of us in our day, but various religious orders requiring people to take solemn vows have existed for a very long time. These have been communities under a "religious" rule. In Genesis 14's case, it was the King of Righteous – the King of Salem – Noah's Son Righteous Son's Rule.

Just as the Order of Saint John is an order of chivalry, so is the Order of Melchizedek an order of perfection. If one studies all the occurrences of the word "perfection" and "perfect" in Scripture, you get a clear picture of the Most High God's Order of Perfection. Being made perfect is all about ACTION!!! The Order of Melchizedek is about completion, fulfilling, consummating, accomplishing, making perfect. It's about being complete in labor, complete in growth, complete in mental character, complete in moral character, a full age man, a mature man. It's about setting out to being made into the exact same image as Yeshua (Jesus).

If Yeshua - the Mature Head of the Body of Christ – is a High Priest made after the Order of Melchizedek, what do you think the priestly role of the Mature Body of Christ is, if we are ONE? *"I in them, and You in Me (Father), that they may be made PERFECT IN ONE; and that the world may know that You (Father) has sent Me, and has loved them, as You love Me"* (John 17.23).

We will do what Yeshua did… walk in the same manner as HE did as a High Priest of the Order of Melchizedek, which does not replace Yeshua being the Highest Priest of the Order of Melchizedek. The Priesthood of All Believers is made up of High Priests of the Order of Melchizedek. Know that this Eternal Priesthood is not based on a person's ancestry, but *"on the basis of the power of an indestructible life. For it is declared: 'You are a priest forever, in the order of Melchizedek' (Hebrews 7.16-17).*

Let's explore some practical points about how a High Priest walked:

" ¹ We have such a HIGH PRIEST WHO IS SEATED AT THE RIGHT HAND OF THE THRONE OF THE MAJESTY IN THE HEAVENS, ["And has raised us together, and made us sit together in heavenly places in Christ Jesus " (Eph 2.6)] *² a Minister of the SANCTUARY and of the TRUE TABERNACLE which the Lord erected, and not man. ³ For every High Priest is appointed to offer both gifts and sacrifices. Therefore, it is necessary that this One also have something to offer. ⁴ For if He were on earth, He would not be a priest, since there are priests who offer the gifts according to the law; ⁵ who serve the copy and shadow of the heavenly things, as Moses was divinely instructed when he was about to make the tabernacle. For He said, 'See that you make all things according to the pattern shown you on the mountain.' ⁶ But now He has obtained a more excellent ministry, inasmuch as He is also Mediator of a better covenant, which was established on better promises" (Hebrews 8.1-6* NKJV*).*

We will be talking about this better covenant and the restoration of all things today.

Clement of Alexandria records: "The knowledge of things past, present and future is revealed by the Son of God, the Great High Priest who passes through the curtain."

Are you a Son of God? Hebrews 7.3 tells us that Melchizedek is made like unto the Son of God. Hint: Study "Son of God" in Scripture!

Do you pass through the curtain (ascend and descend)? The Biblical Pattern of the Pattern Son after His crucifixion was first Jesus descended (taking captivity captive), then ascended on high. Remember that "Spirit is already seated in heaven and is here on earth within you. We are already simultaneously there, here and everywhere. [He has set eternity in our hearts. The whole universe can't contain God, but He is within you]. Spirit is like mixing two glasses of water together. Your eyes are simply opening up to [the eternal] reality, which is I AM seeing who I AM already" (Belle Twigg 10-12-2015).

YESHUA was a man on earth and divine in the heavenlies… that's who I AM is. Your cherubic nature simply is stepping into the reality of who you are (past the constraints of this world). *"So God created man in His own image, in the image of God" (Genesis 1.27).* Never forget that you have been made in God's own image. That means that your original pattern is divine. Don't settle for anything less in your journey to be just like Yeshua back to Eden and beyond. "Manifesting your cherubic nature" or "taking on your cherubic nature" is about constantly abiding in Him in heaven and earth [multiplicity within us body, soul and spirit in union with the divine nature]. We become so able to reflect Him that we become who we truly are supposed to be. We are the reflection formed out of His Spirit, becoming the Son of God on earth [Hebrews 7.3 – *Great Tsadik*]. The *Great Tsadik* – those in the Order of Melchizedek made like unto the Son of God - take on the divine nature of God; this is where the Hebrews teach that we take on the Thirteen Attributes of God, which are not forced... a flowing steam of living water (Exodus 34.6-7).

According to Exodus 26.31, the Veil was woven from fine linen, plus blue, purple and scarlet thread (assumption is wool... essence of a lamb). It was *hoseb*, i.e., skilled work.

Both Philo and Josephus record what was believed about the VEIL in the first-century – the time of Yeshua. The four colors represented the four elements from which the world was made:

1)   Red, being fire.

2)   Blue, being air.

3)   Purple, being water.

4)   White, being the earth.

The Mishnah (Jewish Commentary) says that the Veil was woven by young women. It measured 20x40 cubits (approximately 10-20 meters). The veil was woven from the four elements, which concealed the glory of God. One side represents matter – the stuff that our three-dimensional visible creation is made of – and the other side is eternity.

The outer vestment of the High Priest was made out of the same fabric as the Veil, which he wore in the Holy Place or

Inner Court. By the way, in the Holy of Holies, the High Priest wore the white linen of the angels.

The colored vestments (garments) therefore are associated with the High Priest's role in our visible creation. Josephus and Philo reveal that the outer garment represented the created world. A century before the first century of Philo and Josephus, the Book of the *Wisdom of Solomon* states in chapter 18, verse 24: *"On Aaron's robe the whole world was depicted."* Thus, the High Priest was an angel (i.e., angelic priest) who emerged from the Holy of Holies into visible creation and clothed himself in the stuff of creation.

Our physical reality of time and space is only on one side of the VEIL. The colored vestment is associated with the High Priest's role in visible creation is equivalent to the place where we practically walk out the Order of Melchizedek.

PLEASE NOTE: The only difference between the fabric of the Veil and the fabric of the High Priest's Outer Garment was/is the Cherubim figures embroidered on the Veil (Exodus 26.31; Exodus 36.25). The image of the Cherubim was woven both on the Tabernacle's ten curtains (its one wall) as well as on the Veil. In Hebrew, the Veil is known as the *Paroches*, which means life. Did you know that only three of the four faces of the Living Creatures of Ezekiel 1 (called Cherubim in Ezekiel 10) - lion, eagle and ox – were embroidered in the Tabernacle? Where was the man?

The Man – the High Priest - had to be transfigured into the image of the Living Creature/Cherubim with the four faces of God – lion, ox, eagle, and man – to walk through the veil. Those who pass beyond the Veil find themselves outside time – the eternal realm. We are told that when Rabbi Ishmael ascended and looked back, he saw the curtain (Veil) on which was depicted past, present and future.

"All generations to the end of time were printed on the curtain of the Omnipresent One. I saw them all with my own eyes" (3 Enoch 45.6).

The *Apocalypse of Abraham (21.1)* describes how the patriarch ascended, and then looked down and saw all creation foreshadowed on the firmament.

Not only can we think of the Holy Place as the earthly realm *("on earth")* and the Holy of Holies as the heavenly eternal realm *("as it is in heaven")*, the Veil can also be thought of as a portal between heaven and earth. Walking back and forth (or simultaneously), which forms an arc between heaven and earth.

There's also an arc between heaven and earth between your two ears. When the High Priest functioned in our visible creation, he wore the sacred name YHVH on his forehead, because he represented the Lord of Hosts dwelling with His people. "Blessed is he who comes with/in the Name of the Lord."

The Veil and the High Priest's outer garment being made

of identical fabric is key to the concept of Incarnation (being begotten) – both Yeshua's Incarnation (who is the Mature Head of the Body of Christ) and His Mature Body (you and me). The vested High Priest in the Temple was the Glory of the Lord veiled in matter.

The greatest detailed account of a connection between the Veil and Incarnation is in the *Infancy Gospel of James* [Apocryphal New Testament]. This early Christian text depicts Mary as one of the young women chosen to weave the new temple Veil. Mary was given purple and red wool to spin [i.e., water and fire]. As she was working, the angel Gabriel spoke to her. Thus Mary (Jesus's earthly mother and part of the pure and spotless Bride) was making the new temple Veil while pregnant. It's possible this is just an early legend that links the incarnation to the veil, but note that Herod was refurbishing the Temple at that time. It's entirely possible that Mary had been a Temple Weaver working on the New Veil.

Luke used Temple Imagery when he described the ascension of Christ as the Great High Priest returning to the Holy of Holies. When Yeshua blessed the disciples, He was taken into heaven by a cloud. In the Temple, the High Priest entered the Holy of Holies surrounded by a cloud or vapor or incense. The ascension of Yeshua ha Machiach was the moment when Jesus passed from one particular time and space in visible creation back into the Holy of Holies – the eternal presence beyond the VEIL.

In the eternal presence beyond the Veil – in the Holy of Holies - was the Word in the beginning, and that very Word was with God, and God was that Word. In the Holy Place (on earth) the Word became flesh and dwelt among us … the first-born of the Father, full of grace and truth.

Let's talk about this fullness of Christ – the fullness of grace and truth - fullness of the very Word in the beginning. We will do what Yeshua did – walk in the same manner as HE did as a High Priest of Order of Melchizedek. The first time the "Order of Melchizedek" is mentioned is in the enthronement set in the Holy of Holies in *The LORD has sworn, and will not lie, You are a priest for ever after the Order of Melchizedek" (Psalm 110.4)*. The Hebrew word for ORDER here is *dib-raw'*. It is made up of the essence of four Hebrew Living Letters: *dalet* (door), *bet* (house), *reysh* (head), *hei* (arms raised with open window over priest's head). The Ancient Hebrew Word Picture (pictograph) for DIB-RAW' ORDER reverberates with an ancient call: "Come! Let's see the most important path for God's family. The ancient "order" in the Order of Melchizedek reveals the Word who is the House Ruler who sets the House Rules for the highest way of life for a person." The very root of the word ORDER in the "Order of Melchizedek" is the Hebrew word *Davar* DAW-BAR' (דבר). It literally means a "word."

There are many dimensions to the gospel being "the word" – a frequency.

The words in Hebrew used to describe a divine command in the first five books in the Bible (Torah):

[1] *mitzvah* – commandment or literally "love deed"

[2] *dibbur* – word

[3] *mishpat* – law

[4] *ed* – testimonial

[5] *chok* – decree or boundary, or literally "engraving"

The LORD wanted me to focus on the importance of ASCENSION DECREES in our heaven-to-earth high priesthood reality walk, which will restore all things:

Notice that a decree is a boundary or an engraving.

"Statutes" is an interesting word as well. Statutes literally mean "something engraved." "To violate statutes" literally means "they have gone through the engraved thing." These engraved things were the divine planes and boundaries set up in the Holy of Holies before the three-dimensional world – visible creation – was made.

The priestly covenant (i.e., Everlasting Covenant) manifests itself as laws and statutes. When they are broken, we are told that the earth withers away and the creation collapses. The LORD gave Phineas and his descendants "My Covenant of Shalom… the Covenant of the Priesthood of

Eternity (or the Covenant of the Eternal Priesthood) because he... made at-one-ment (atonement) for the people of Is-real (Numbers 25.12-13).

The Covenant of Peace was linked exclusively to the High Priesthood and entailed making atonement to repair any breach in the Covenant of Shalom, which exposed the people to danger. Those who break the Eternal Covenant have gone through the laws (i.e., broken through and destroyed on earth what had been engraved in the Holy of Holies). *"On earth, as it is in heaven"* is a good description of creation as it is intended to be. Keep in mind that the crux of the restoration of all things has to do with the Priesthood of Eternity restoring His engraved things.

During a *Mystic Mentoring Group Ascension*, we asked if we could deal with the corruption of the Colorado Presidential Primary. We laid it on His Altar and focused on the Father's Perfect Will. What He did went beyond what we could think or imagine (still today). We were led to reset an engraving. This particular engraving involved all creation's pledge of allegiance to YHVH... one dominion under the Almighty God, indivisible, with love, liberty and justice for all. We were also led to break the power of corruption from all legislative bodies in all creation.

Shall we dive a little deeper?

Proverbs 8.27-29 is Wisdom's description of the sequence of Creation, since she had been in the beginning – in the Holy of Holies – besides Creator God. The vision in

Proverbs 8 is like Genesis 1, except that Wisdom had been beside the Creator when He engraved a circle on the face of the deep, when He set for the sea its engraved mark… when He engraved the foundations of the earth … the engraved state preceded (or lays beneath) the material world.

Jeremiah knew that the sea had an engraving of eternity it could not pass (Jeremiah 5.22). He knew that there were ENGRAVINGS for the moon and the stars (Jeremiah 31.35-36). Everything we know, see, and experience in this world has its engraved place and its limit… *Job 14.5* speaks of people's engraving: *"You have made his engraving and he cannot pass it." Job 23.14* speaks of *"He will complete what is ENGRAVED for me."*

Psalm 2.7 KJV – *"I will declare the DECREE (chok –* boundary – decree – literally engraving): *the LORD has said unto me, Thou art My Son; this day have I begotten thee."* The literal translation of *Psalm 2.7* is *"I will tell of my engraving (or, the engraving). The Lord said to me: You are My son, today I have begotten you."*

Clement of Alexandria taught that the Son had been drawn in outline in the beginning – a state of existence which preceded solidity and matter. According to 3 Enoch 39.1-2, the Throne of God – Throne of Glory – was engraved with names, and when they flew off, these engravings became angels. One of the sins of the fallen angels seems to have been reducing humans from living beings to human beings … from their angelic state to that of mortals.

Our divine cherubic nature – being made in God's image –
is engraved on His Throne of Glory, and when our
frequency aligns with His, we resonate at 144,000 cycles per
second (cps), which is the base frequency of all pervading
light in the cosmos – all of creation, which is our
primordial state before the Fall with all Twelve Strands of
our DNA turned on as a light antenna. When we are
completely turned on, vibrating at 144,000 cps base
frequency of light, we literally become His exact image (are
begotten). We fill out the engraving of God's Son's Body
[corporate and individual work], flying off His Throne of
Glory to rule and reign in complete harmony with the
Father, as one of His Chariot Thrones.

Divine Cherubic Nature – Enoch was transformed into an
angel, resurrected, and sent back to earth. The Book of
Second Enoch chapter 22 reveals Enoch as a High Priest
who ascended to heaven to stand before the Throne of
God. There the LORD summons the Archangel Michael to
remove Enoch's earthly clothing (mortal body) and to dress
him in the garments of glory, which was his resurrected
body. [During the MM Group Ascension on April 30,
2016, we received this same Robe of Immortality.] In the
language of the Heavenly Temple, resurrection was/is a
theosis – transformation of a human being into divine
being… not a post-mortem experience. After Michael
dressed Enoch in garments of glory (i.e., Robes of
Immortality), Enoch was anointed with fragrant myrrh oil
and Enoch saw himself transform into an angel. Myrrh oil
is used to consecrate high priests and the furnishings of the

Tabernacle. No wonder early Christians thought of themselves as angels on earth!

According to the Enochic tradition, the Eternal Covenant had been broken as the result of corrupted knowledge. It was the abuse of knowledge and the power it gave that destroyed the Eternal Covenant and fragmented creation.

The fullest picture of the Eternal Covenant is found in the Book of First Enoch. The context of this poem is how the fallen angels corrupted the creation, the power of the Great Oath, and how it had been broken:

"These are the secrets of this OATH:

The heaven was suspended before the creation of the world and for ever.

And through it the earth was founded upon the water...

From the creation of the world and unto eternity.

And through that OATH the sea was created,

and He set the sand against the time of anger

And it dare not pass beyond it from the creation of the world unto eternity

And through that OATH the depths are made fast...

And through that OATH the sun and moon complete their course...

And through the OATH the stars complete their course…"

(1 Enoch 69.16).

All the things created on Day One in the Holy of Holies was a process of binding into bonds, engraving limits and definitions, and then using them to order the visible creation. This shall you, as priests of the Eternal Covenant, do too. The Kingdom of God, which Jesus speaks of… is the state of the Holy of Holies… the unity at the heart of all things, which secures the Eternal Covenant. Holy Royal Priests and Kings of the Order of Melchizedek are restoring all things. We are putting creation back together again by making fractured people and pieces whole again.

Hebrews 7 speaks of being made a priest after the Order of Melchizedek with an OATH (Hebrews 7.20).

Let's read some sections of *Hebrew 7.19-28*:

19 For the law made nothing PERFECT, but there has come in its place a better hope, by which we draw near to God.

20 And He confirmed it with an OATH.

21 For they were made priests [Levitical/Aaronic] *without OATHS; but THIS ONE WAS MADE A PRIEST WITH AN OATH, as it was said concerning Him by David, The LORD has sworn, and will not lie, Thou art a priest forever after the Order of Melchizedek…*

24 Because He is IMMORTAL [CONTINUES FOREVER], *He has a priesthood which remains forever* [AN UNCHANGEABLE PRIESTHOOD]…

28 For the law appoints imperfect men priests; but THE WORD OF THE OATH which comes after the law APPOINTS THE SON WHO IS [CONSECRATED] *PERFECT FOREVERMORE."*

Through the Word of the Oath, sons of the Living God made like unto Melchizedek take on the very DNA of God. They are made after the IMMORTAL PRIESTHOOD with the OATH OF THE ETERNAL COVENANT. These are priests forever after the Order of Melchizedek.

There is an unchangeable agreement to the heirs of promise sealed with an UNCHANGEABLE, ENGRAVED OATH where He has literally set eternity in our hearts.

2 – SHEKINAH SABBATH

There are profound mysteries hidden in the Lord's Temple where the priests of the Most High God sing their Sabbath Day songs to Melchizedek. Before we plumb the depths of the Sabbath Songs sung to Melchizedek, let's first delve into the Sabbath.

Hebrew Mysticism speaks of: "The sanctity of the Sabbath as long as it lasts imposes ABSOLUTE REST both in the higher and lower worlds, during which the punishments of the wicked cease and their overlookers remain inactive until the children of Israel have finished reciting the words: *'Blessed art Thou oh Lord who separates the holy from the unholy.'*"

From *An introduction to Shekhinah: the divine feminine*: Sabbath rituals allude to the Shekhinah (Divine Essence of God). It's understood that each action taken in the material world (in the earth below) has a direct effect on heavenly matters (heaven above). Shifrah bas Joseph (a woman) redefined many daily roles of women, particularly on Sabbath. For instance, the Sabbath evening candle-lighting ritual, for

19

which women had previously been assigned the role of candle-lighting because Eve reputedly snuffed out the light of God by sinning, she redefined it as: "Because the Shelter of Peace (The People of Israel as the Embodiment of the Shekhinah) rests on us (women) during the Sabbath, on the (Sabbath-) souls, it is therefore proper for us to do below, in this form, as it is done above (within the Godhead), to kindle the lights. Therefore, because the two souls shine on the Sabbath, they (women) must light two candles... Therefore, by kindling the lamps for the holy Sabbath, we awaken great arousal in the upper world..." [Think of intimacy with the Heavenly Bridegroom and His Bride]. By identifying with the divine essence of God (Shekinah), and achieving unity with the divine itself *(Ein Sof)*, we each seek to lift the Shekinah, and restore unity within the Divine.

Notice the *Shekinah* is a she. Shekinah has a feminine essence. We are going to be speaking about the Bride of Christ a lot today. Why are we speaking about a feminine entity – the Bride of Christ – when we are exploring various MEL GEL facets?

FOR REFERENCE SAKE: I corporately ascended pretty much every week with a group of four people for four years. We received divine revelation about both Order of Melchizedek and the Bride of Christ at the same time. I was confused. I had questions like: Is the Order of Melchizedek and the Bride the same thing in the spirit? I sought HIM persistently for months and one day a one-liner came: "Melchizedek is the predecessor of the Bride." Melchizedek prepares the Bride. You as a royal Melchizedek priest prepares your own inner fire bride, whose purpose is to become just like Jesus (Yeshua) and be ONE (unite) with the Divine – YHVH. The Order of Melchizedek is like the Queen's Guard (the Bride of Christ's Guard). When I've corporately ascended and the Melchizedek element has been part of the Group Ascension, it has always been militaristic; therefore, many times I will call the Order of Melchizedek – the Melchizedek Army.

The mysteries associated with Shekinah are also delved into in *Sapphire Throne Ministries'* second *UNLOCKING MELCHIZEDEK* video available on YouTube, which is entitled - King of Salem. Check it out => https://www.youtube.com/watch?v=QkipeFOCQr4. Melchizedek is called the King of Righteousness as w ell as the King of Peace (i.e., Salem). The title King of Salem can also mean Perfect King where a king rules perfectly according to the dictates of YHVH's heart. Melchizedek, as the King of Peace, symbolizes Shekinah, which is both known as *Malkut* (Kingdom) and *Tsedeq* (Righteousness). Shekinah is a dwelling presence. We are told by Christian Mystics that Shekinah is not found among sinners, and it's a divine rainbow that radiates colors in two directions. This hints to a higher reality where those in the Order of Melchizedek, as Shekinah, is *shalem*. They are perfect and complete when they have been made into the exact same image as Yeshua Messiah – the High Priest of the Order of Melchizedek. This allows these ones to unite to the higher divine energy (or life force) that empowers them to rule and reign in Christ.

If you were with us for the first MEL GEL Class, we spoke about WISDOM and her testimony of creation as she stood beside the Creator. In Proverbs 8, Wisdom speaks of the engravings. Recall that the engraved things were the divine plans and boundaries set up in the Holy of Holies before visible creation was made. Also, recall that the Covenant of Peace is the Eternal Covenant. It's the Covenant of the Eternal Priesthood who is the King of Peace… the righteous king radiating His divine rainbow colors, sound waves, frequencies, vibrations and energies… radiating His Shekinah Presence Glory.

Let's sit at the feet of Wisdom to learn more about being Kings of Peace… Kings of Shekinah… Kings of the Shekinah Sabbath.

The First Temple has always been remembered as the True Temple that Moses made in the exact pattern he saw in the heaven. In the time of the Messiah, five things would be restored which had been in the First Temple but not in the Second: the fire (on God's Altar), the Golden Menorah, the Ark of the Covenant (Ark of His Presence) with a blue flame on top of it, the Spirit of the Living God, and the Cherubim according to the Jewish Commentary *Numbers Rabbah XV.10*.

These five elements are being restored again in this Kingdom Day again by the mature Body of Christ who will attach to the Mature Head of Christ – Yeshua. [The Spirit of the Living God will lead the Cherubim (Living Creature, One New Man in Christ made after the Order of Melchizedek to the heavenly Temple where the fire in the Outer Court represents the lowest level where Group Ascensions can go… the fire in the inner Court (Holy Place) – Golden Menorah – signifies the next highest place groups can ascend to (with their souls and spirits)… the blue flame fire over the Ark of the Presence is the highest place a group ascension can go. There are many names for this place… The Great Blue, The Sapphire Cube, The New Jerusalem, etc.]

The First Temple was also the House of Wisdom. The traditional Jewish Commentary *Genesis Rabbah XLIII.6* states that the bread which Melchizedek brought to Abraham was the Bread of the Presence, and there follows a reference to a passage in Proverbs 9 about Wisdom's Table. In Proverbs 9.5-6 we find that Wisdom has invited her devotees to her table. "Come, eat of my bread and drink of the wine I have mixed. Leave simpleness, and live, and walk in the way of discernment." Wisdom presided over a table where bread and wine was taken. By taking her bread and wine, Wisdom's devotees acquired LIFE and WISDOM.

Jeremiah 7.18 KJV says: *"The children gather wood, and the fathers kindle the fire, and the women knead their dough, to make cakes to the Queen of Heaven, and to pour out drink offerings UNTO OTHER GODS, that they provoke me to anger."* The bread and wine of the Babylonian (false) Queen of Heaven in this verse are merely a twisted counterfeit of a righteous real. There was, and still is, a multi-member True Queen of Heaven who offers the Bread of The Presence and the Drink Offering of the most fine wine to the One True and Living God. The exact same priestly protocols for the Table of Showbread in the First Temple are the same worship protocols for the True Queen of Heaven. On the gold table was placed plates and dishes for incense (frankincense), flagons (a large container in which drink is served, typically with a handle and spout... used to hold the wine for the Eucharist – Blood of Christ), and bowls for libations as well as the Bread of the Presence (Exodus 25.29). By the way, the process of baking the Bread of The Presence was a family secret of the House of Garmu... and they truly kept their secret. [*Mishnah Yoma 3.11*].

Since gold signifies the Most Holy things in the Temple, we can say that the Bread of the Presence acquired holiness while in the Temple. *The Targum* [which is an ancient Aramaic paraphrase or interpretation of the Hebrew Bible, of a type made from about the first-century AD when Hebrew was declining as a spoken language... *Targum Onkelos Lev 24.9*] describes the Bread of the Presence as the most sacred of all the offerings. It was described as the Most Holy portion for the High Priests [recall from the first Mel Gel Class that we are one with Jesus – Yeshua the High Priest of the Order of Melchizedek – and therefore function as High Priests too... The pattern is that there is only one High Priest], which means that it imparted holiness to them (Lev 24.9), and it was eaten by them each

Sabbath when the new loaves of bread were taken into the Temple.

The "righteous real" here is not that the Queen of Heaven was worshipped with incense, libations of wine and bread, but SHE worshipped Creator God whom SHE (WISDOM as our prototype here) stands alongside. You can find references that the communion elements represent the Queen of Heaven, because when set righteously up-right we understand that SHE (you and I) are one with Jesus Christ (Yeshua Messiah) ... bone of His bone and flesh of His flesh... never ever replace the centrality of Jesus Christ and His sacrifice on the Cross, which communion represents.

The Bread of the Presence is the *Panim* Bread, which literally means "faces" in Hebrew.

Did you know that the four living creatures (which comprise only one "Living Creature" ... check out the transition in Ezekiel 1.20) each containing the Four Faces of God is actually a feminine form? The only English version that attempts to translate the confusing Hebrew of Ezekiel 1 and 10, and gives a fair representation of what Ezekiel literally communicated is the AV.

Question: What is the AV (Authorized Version) of the Bible? Answer: The King James Version (KJV) is also known as the Authorized Version (AV) or King James Bible(KJB), an English translation of the Christian Bible for the Church of England begun in 1604 and completed in 1611.

In the King James Authorized Version of the Bible, Ezekiel (who was a priest in the First Temple and deported to Babylon) describes how the lady left the Temple.

There are, in fact, four feminine Living Creatures in human form (Ezekiel 1.5) and they each have four faces (presences), wings, wheels and hands. In the midst of the Living Ones is a fire. Her essence (the spirit of the Living Creature [feminine singular] is in the wheels (Ezekiel 1.20). Over the heads (plural) of the Living Creature (feminine singular), there is the likeness of terrible crystal or a firmament. Above that, there's a Throne with a human form of One Burning Man (One New Man in Christ) sitting on it with the likeness of the Rainbow Shekinah Glory of God above (Ezekiel 1.28).

So we have a four-fold fiery female figure, and the sound of her voice was "like the voice of *El Shaddai*" (the many-breasted All-Sufficient Almighty God – Ezekiel 1.24; 10.5). In Ezekiel chapter 10, Ezekiel describes the glory leaving the Temple in verse 10: *"As for their appearances, they four had one likeness, as if a wheel had been in the midst of a wheel" (AV).* *"All their body* [singular "body" and plural suffix] *was full of pints of light" (Ezekiel 10.12). "She is the Living One that I saw beneath the God of Israel by the River Chebar" (Ezekiel 10.20).*

Ben Sira, a Jewish Scribe who wrote four centuries after Ezekiel's vision described Wisdom as the one who served in the Temple of Zion. She is the High Priest of Zion (Ben

Sira 24.10).

Another great symbol of Wisdom is the Tree of Life. *Proverbs 3.18 — "She is a Tree of Life to those who lay hold of her; those who hold fast to her are happy."* Read Proverbs 3.13-20.

Enoch reveals more about the Giant Tree. Enoch saw a great tree by the throne on a visionary journey in heaven *"whose fragrance was beyond all fragrance, and whose leaves and blossoms never wither or rot" (1 Enoch 24.4)*. Mere mortals cannot touch this Great Tree until after the Great Judgment, when its fruit would be given to the chosen ones, and the Tree itself would be transplanted again into the Temple. Enoch also reveals in *2 Enoch 8.4* that this Tree of Life is the place the Lord rests when He is in Paradise. *"I saw Paradise, and in the midst, the Tree of Life, at that place where the Lord takes His rest when He goes [up] to Paradise... that tree is indescribable for pleasantness and fragrance, and more beautiful than any created thing. Its appearance is gold and crimson and with the form of fire."*

In an account of Adam and Eve written at the end of the Second Temple period [*Apocalypse of Moses 22*], when God returns to Paradise, the Chariot Throne rests at the Tree of Life and all the flowers come into bloom.

The only tree in the earthly temple is the Golden Menorah – the Tree of Life - which is a Tree of Fire that uses oil to let there be light.

The oil that anointed the Royal High Priest of God's Temple, and made him ... the Child of Wisdom... the Son of God who was perfumed with oil from the Tree of Life. Wisdom has been described by Ben Sira as the oil itself: a sweet perfume of myrrh, cinnamon and olive oil (Ben Sira 24.15) as prescribed in the instructions for the Tabernacle in Exodus 30.23-25.

Do you remember from our first MEL GEL Class that Enoch had the experience of being anointed with this oil of wisdom from the Tree of Life? *2 Enoch 22* tells us: *"The LORD said to Michael: 'Go and take Enoch from his earthly clothing* [from his fallen mortal body]. *And so Michael did just as the LORD commanded him. He anointed me and he clothed me, and the appearance of that oil is greater than the greatest light, and its ointment is like sweet dew* [the symbol of resurrection] *and its fragrance is myrrh, and it is like the rays of the glittering sun. And I looked at myself and I had become like one of the glorious ones.' "* Immediately, Enoch began to see the six days of creation after this."

Know that the myrrh oil is a sacrament of *theosis*… an outward act and visible sign of an inward and spiritual divine grace. In this case the visible thing associated with *theosis* is myrrh oil. *Theosis* is defined as "the understanding that human beings can have real union with God, and so become like God to such a degree that we participate in the divine nature."

Recall from MEL GEL #1: In the language of the Heavenly Temple, resurrection was/is a *theosis* – transformation of a human being into a divine being… it is NOT something that happens after you die and go to heaven.

The perfumed myrrh anointing oil was kept in the Holy of Holies (in eternity outside time), and when a Royal High Priest was anointed, we are told that he received the gift of wisdom herself: resurrection life, vision, knowledge and true wealth. The High Priest was anointed on his head and between his eyelids, which symbolized the opening of his eyes. In the time of Josiah, the oil was hidden away and the priests lost their vision.

Memories of the precious gift of Wisdom in the fragrant myrrh oil appear in several early Christian texts:

- In the first letter that the Beloved Apostle John wrote: *"You have the chrism from the Holy One and you know all things … You have no need for anyone to teach you anything"* (1 John 2.20, 27).

- The collection of early Christian hymns known as *The Odes of Solomon 11 and 36* includes: *"My eyes were enlightened and my face received the dew, and my soul was refreshed with the pleasant fragrance of the LORD"* and *"He anointed me with His perfection and I became as one of those who are near Him."* A Dead Sea Scroll from Cave 11, Manuscript 13 – 11Q13 – speaks of a Melchizedek Company of a congregation of Sons of Righteousness that *"stand in the council of God."* It's spoken of in *Psalm 82.1 – "A godlike being"* [mature sons who are "living creatures" made after the Order of

Melchizedek who together make up a feminine Living Creature – the Bride of Christ] *"has taken his place in the council of God in the midst of the divine beings he holds judgment."*

- In *Clementine Recognitions 1.45-46,* Clement speaks of an explanation of the word "Christ" ascribed to the Apostle Peter: *"The Son of God, the beginning of all things, became man. He was the first whom God anointed with oil taken from the wood of the Tree of Life."* Peter spoke of how Christ would, in turn, anoint those who enter the Kingdom of God with the oil from the Tree of Life.

- Peter continued: *"Aaron the first High Priest was anointed with a composition of CHRISM which was made after the pattern of the spiritual ointment."* If the earthly copy was so transformative and powerful, how much greater was the CHRISM extracted from the very branch of the Tree of Life.

Myrrh oil was used in the Temple to anoint high priests to make or to declare them sacred as well as to dedicate them for divine purpose… a divine ordination, if you will. Enoch had an other-worldly experience as a High Priest who ascended to heaven to stand before the Throne of God, who was transformed into an angel, resurrected, and sent back to earth. His *theosis* was complete when he was anointed with myrrh oil. The myrrh oil is for *"the elect and righteous who will be living in the day of tribulation, when all the wicked and godless people are to be removed (from the earth) ... a remote* [generation] *which is to come" according to 1 Enoch 1.1-2:*

> *1 Enoch 1.7: "And the earth shall be completely torn apart, and all that is on the earth shall be destroyed, and there shall be a judgment on all."*

> *Revelation 21.7-8: " ⁷ He who overcomes will inherit all this, and I will be his God and he will be my son. ⁸ But the cowardly, the unbelieving, the vile, the murderers, the sexually immoral, those who practice magic arts, the idolaters and all liars – their place will be in the fiery lake of burning sulfur. This is the second death."*

> *1 Enoch 1.8: "But the righteous He will make peace; and will protect the elect and mercy shall be on them. And they shall all belong to God, and they shall prosper, and they shall be blessed. And the light of God shall shine on them."*

> *Revelation 21.23-24: "²³ The city does not need the sun or the moon to shine on it, for the glory of God gives it light, and the Lamb is its lamp. ²⁴ The nations will walk by its light, and the kings of the earth will bring their splendor into it."*

Notice that the very first chapter of 1 Enoch lines up with Revelation chapter 21, which has to do with the sons' Bride of Christ:

> *"He that overcomes shall inherit all things; and I will be his God, and he shall be my son" (Revelation 21.7 ₖⱼᵥ).* In Greek, *huios* sons [pronounced we-os] are mature

sons: *"Though He* [Jesus] *was a Son* [Huios], *yet He learned obedience by the things which He suffered"* (Hebrews 5.8)...

Physical Growth is a function of time.

Intellectual Growth is a function of learning.

Spiritual Growth is a function of obedience *(Hebrews 5.8-10; 1 Peter 1:22).*

Immature sons in the Greek is *teknon.* These are three things immature sons do:

[1]   Less likely to follow the leading of the Spirit of God (i.e., have not yet learned to act only on Spirit's leading).

[2]   Most often react or respond emotionally or intellectually to circumstances they face.

[3]   Seek to protect themselves; therefore: *"always learning and never able to come to the knowledge of the truth"* (2 Timothy 3.7).

The [feminine] New Living Creature in Christ manifesting in our day is made up of mature sons of God that can and will do nothing of themselves. They will do only what they see the Father doing (John 5.19). BTW - This is the meaning of A BODY PREPARED: *"To do Thy will, O God"* (Hebrews 10.5-7).

Remember Mature Sons of Most High God are the predecessors (who prepare) the Bride for Divine Union in which this Pure and Spotless One will be His Helpmate: *"Come, I will show you The Bride, the wife of the Lamb"* (Revelation 21.9b).

"¹And I saw a new heaven and a new earth; for the first heaven and the first earth had passed away; and the sea was no more. ²And I saw the holy city, New Jerusalem, coming down from God, prepared as a Bride adorned for her husband. ³And I heard a great voice from heaven saying. Behold, the Tabernacle of God is with men, and He will dwell with them, and they shall be his people, and the very God shall be with them and be their God" (Revelation 21.1-3 _{Aramaic}).

The idea that God dwells in man and that man is His Temple is merely another way to portray the Shekinah Presence of God resting on man (Revelation 21.3). Traditionally, Hebrews understood that the Sabbath surrounds you wherever you go.

The word *shekinah* itself is not found in Scripture, but the concept clearly is. Most believe that the term *shekinah* was coined as a noun through a derivation of the Hebrew verb *shakan*, which is used to describe the "abiding, dwelling, or habitation" of the physical manifestations of God (Exodus 24.16; Exodus 40.35; Numbers 9.16-18). The word *shekinah* is used to describe the mystical *shekinah* presence in the Tabernacle. When the Hebrew word *Mishkan* (Tabernacle) is used, it is understood to be a derivation of *shakan*, which is the "dwelling place" of the Divine Presence of God and His Cosmic Glory, or we can simply say: *Shekinah*.

The Hebrew verb *shakan* (שָׁכַן) simply means to take up residence for a long time in a neighborhood. It's a protracted dwelling in the midst of a neighborhood or a group of people. *Shakan*'s primary meaning is to reside and continue as a member of the community.

The *Shekinah* Presence was not God, but an ethereal (yet physical) manifestation of His actual presence among His people. The *Shekinah* Presence appears to be first evident in Scripture in the crossing of the Red Sea where the pillar of fire by night and the pillar of cloud by day that protected them from the pursuing Egyptians. To this day, the *Shekinah* is believed to be a protection in the case of the nightly prayer of the Hebrews: "on my four sides angels, and above my head the Shekinah of God" (comp. Kid. 31a).

The nation of Israel was led by the *Shekinah* for forty years. Then the Holy Presence of the Omniscient God inhabited the Wilderness Tabernacle and Solomon's Temple (i.e., the First Temple).

Earlier, Moses, Aaron, and Seventy Elders had gone up into the cloud on Mount Sinai and actually saw the Shekinah glory: *Exodus 24.15-17 – "15And Moses went up into the mount, and a cloud covered the mount. 16And the glory of the LORD* [Kabod YHVH] *abode* [shakan] *upon Mount Sinai and the cloud covered it six days; and the seventh day* [Sabbath day] *He called unto Moses out of the midst of the cloud. 17And the sight of the glory of the LORD* [Kabod YHVH] *was like a devouring fire on the top of the mount in the eyes of the children of Israel."* Remember that *Exodus 24.10-11* relates: " *¹⁰And they saw the God of Israel; and there was under His feet as it were a paved work of a sapphire stone, and as it were the body of heaven in his clearness. ¹¹And upon the nobles of the children of Israel he laid not a hand; also they saw God, and did eat and drink."*

NOTE: *Shekinah* in Hebrew (just like the Living Creature(s)) is a feminine word. Some hold that the Shekinah represents the feminine attributes of God.

The recurring theme of the Sabbath Bride is best known in the writings and songs of the legendary 16ᵗʰ century mystic, – Rabbi Isaac Luria. Here's a quote from his famous Shabbat hymn:

I sing in hymns

to enter the gates

of the Field

of holy apples.

A new table

we prepare for her,

a lovely candelabra

sheds its light upon us. [sometimes *Shekinah* is associated with "light"]

Between right and left

the Bride approaches

in holy jewels

and festive garments...

When the people of Israel stood before Mount Sinai, the Lord spoke to them: *"Remember that I said to the Sabbath: The Community of Israel is your mate.' Hence: Remember the Sabbath Day to sanctify it"* (Exodus 20.8). "Sanctify" is the Hebrew word *le-kadesh* and means to consecrate a woman... to betroth.

In Abraham Joshua Heschel's classic book *The Sabbath*, he speaks about: "The Sabbath is a Bride, and its celebration is like a wedding. We learn in the Midrash [an ancient commentary about Hebrew Scriptures attached to their biblical text] that the Sabbath is like unto a bride. Just as a bride when she comes to her groom is lovely, bedecked and perfumed, so the Sabbath comes to Israel lovely and perfumed, as it is written: *And on the Seventh Day He ceased from work and He rested (Exodus 31.17)*, and immediately afterward we read: *And He gave unto Moses kekalloto* [the word *kekalloto* means when He finished, but it also means as his bride], to teach us that just as a bride is lovely and bedecked, so is the Sabbath lovely and bedecked; just as a groom is dressed in his finest garments, so is a man on the

Sabbath Day dressed in his finest garments; just as a man rejoices all the days of the wedding feast, so does man rejoice on the Sabbath; just as a groom does no work on his wedding day, so does a man abstain from work on the Sabbath Day; and therefore the Sages and Ancient Saints called the Sabbath a Bride. There is a hint in the Sabbath prayers [for Hebrews]. In the Friday evening service we say *Thou hast sanctified the seventh day*, referring to the marriage of the bride to the groom (sanctification is the Hebrew word for marriage). In the morning prayer we say: *Moses rejoiced in the gift* [of the Sabbath] bestowed upon him which corresponds to the groom's rejoicing with the bride. In the additional prayer we make mention of *the two lambs, the fine flour for a meal offering, mingled with oil and the drink thereof* referring to the meat, the bread, the wine, and the oil used in the wedding banquet. In the last hour of the day we say: *Thou art One* to parallel the consummation of the marriage by which the bride and groom are united."

The Shabbat is both a Queen and a Bride. There is a Jewish tradition called the *Shabbat Kallah* where the Shekinah is equated to the Sabbath Bride, which continues to this day. Symbolically, when God returns to Jerusalem, He remarries Israel. At Sinai, God married Israel with his side of the ketubah (marriage covenant) – the Ten Commandments. It's time for the nation on those who are Is-real to fulfill the other side of the marriage covenant. It's time for the shattered pieces of the Sapphire Cubes to come back together, so we can be betrothed and married… as ONE.

The love poem of God and Israel is called *Lechah Dodi*: *"I am my beloved's, and his desire is for me. Come, my beloved, let us go into the open [L'cha Dodi neitzei ha'sadeh] (Song of Songs 7.11-12).* The term Lechah Dodi is taken from these verses in the Song of Songs. The words are attributed to the wisest man on earth, King Solomon, the builder of the First Temple where the Holy of Holies is called The Oracle and in the midst of it are the figures of two living creatures with four faces (presences).

The Shekinah Sabbath is God's Queen and Bride. Her corporate ascent to the Throne marks her coronation alongside Him. Never ever forget that the SHEKINAH SABBATH BRIDE is the space and place where God's manifest Presence resides among a group of people.

According to the *Jewish Encyclopedia*, the *Shekinah* appears to the pure in heart:

[1] when two are engaged with Torah (the Word of God).

[2] when ten pray. Ten is a governmental number for a *minyan*. The *Jerusalem Talmud* offers two sources for the *miniyan* requirement. Pay attention to the word "congregation."

> [a] *"Speak to all the congregation of the children of Israel, and say to them: You shall be holy" (Leviticus 19.2)* and *"How long shall I bear with this evil congregation which murmur against me?" (Numbers 14.27).* Since the term "congregation" in

the latter verse refers to the ten spies, so does the previous verse: "You shall be holy" refers to a "congregation" of ten.

[b] The second source is based on the term "children of Israel" which appears in the following two verses: *"And I shall be sanctified in the midst of the children of Israel" (Leviticus 22.32);* and *"And the children of Israel came to buy among those that came" (Genesis 42.5).* Just as the "children of Israel" in the later verse refers to the ten sons of Jacob who descended to Egypt to obtain food during the famine, so too the former verse refers to sanctification among the "children of Israel" in the presence of ten.)

[3] when three sit together for righteous judgment.

[4] when the mysticism of the Merkabah is explained.

[5] when studying of the Law at night – Treasure of Darkness… Remember the engravings and the Hebrew words to describe a DIVINE COMMAND? *"Mitzvah"* – commandment or literally love deed, *"Dibbur"* – word, *"Misphat"* – Law *"Ed"* = testimonial, *"chok"* decree, boundary or engraving.

[6] when reading of the Shema – *"Hear O Israel, the LORD (YHVH) our God is one LORD: And you shall love the LORD your God with all your heart, and with all your soul, and with all your might (strength)" (Deuteronomy 6.4-5).*

[7] when operating in hospitality, benevolence, or chastity.

[8] when there is peace and faithfulness in a marriage.

[9] and similar deeds and qualities.

Sin always causes *Shekinah* to depart. Before the Israelites sinned (the sin of the Golden Calf), the *Shekinah* rested on everyone.

3 – SABBATH SACRIFICES AND ABSOLUTE REST

Let's begin with the glorious topic of "Absolute Rest."

Hebrew Mysticism speaks of "The sanctity of the Sabbath as long as it lasts imposes <u>absolute rest</u> both in the higher and lower worlds, during which the punishments of the wicked cease and their overlookers remain inactive until the children of Israel have finished reciting the words: 'Blessed art Thou oh Lord who separates the holy from the unholy.'"

From the *Webster's Collegiate Dictionary (Tenth Edition)*:

> **absolute** ~*noun* a value or principle that is regarded as universally valid or that may be viewed without relation to other things. (e.g., "good and evil are presented as absolutes")

absolute ~*adjective* [1] not qualified or diminished in any way; total (e.g., "absolute secrecy"); *syn* – complete, total, utter, outright entire, perfect, pure. [2] viewed or existing independently and not in relation to other things; not relative or comparative.

rest ~ *noun* [1] an instance or period of relaxing or ceasing to engage in strenuous or stressful activity; *syn* – repose, relaxation, leisure, respite, time off, breathing space, downtime [2] an object that is used to support something (like God Himself on the Sabbath). *"Who is this One ascending from the wilderness in the pillar of the glory cloud?" (Song of Solomon 3.6 Passion Translation). "Who is this that comes up from the wilderness leaning on her beloved?" (Song of Solomon 8.5).*

rest ~ *verb* [1] ease work or movement in order to relax, refresh oneself, or recover strength; syn – relax, ease up, let up, slow down, take a break, unwind, recharge one's batteries, take it easy, put your feet up [2] be placed or supported so as to stay in a specified position; *syn* – lie, be supported by

"But the dove found no REST for the sole of her foot, and she returned unto him into the ark, for the waters were on the face of the whole earth; then he put forth his hand, and took her, and pulled her unto him into the ark" (Genesis 8.9 KJV).

The word "dove" here is a gentle term of endearment. It's the Hebrew word *"yownah"* (pronounced yō·nä'). "Thy eyes are doves," like dove's eyes. The one with dove's eyes – the Sabbath Shekinah – the Sabbath Bride and Queen"

"My beloved spoke, and said to me: "Rise up, my love, my fair one, and come away. For lo, the winter is past, the rain is over and gone. The flowers appear on the earth; the time of singing has come, and the voice of the turtle dove is heard in our land. The fig tree puts forth her green figs, and the vines with the tender grapes give a good smell. Rise up, my love, my fair one, And come away! O my DOVE, in the clefts of the rock, in the secret places of the cliff, let me see your face, let me hear your voice; for your voice is sweet, and your face is lovely" (Song of Solomon 2.10-14 NKJV). Did you know that in the natural doves have no peripheral vision? They can only see directly in front; therefore, doves are representative of focus.

"The Beloved – *I have come to My garden, My sister, My spouse; I have gathered My myrrh with My spice; I have eaten my honeycomb with My honey* [Honey Tree is the Tree of Life, which if you recall, is the place the Lord rests when He is in Paradise. The *Merkabah* (Chariot Throne) also rests at the Tree of Life and all the flowers come into bloom – "The flowers appear on the earth" (SS 2.12)]; *I have drunk My wine with My milk. (To His Friends) Eat, O friends! Drink, yes, drink deeply, O beloved ones!* The Shulamite - *I sleep, but my heart is awake; it is the voice of my Beloved! He knocks, saying, 'Open for me, My sister, My love, My DOVE, My perfect* one [the one who has perfected their own inner fire bride]; *for My head is covered with dew,* [Psalm 133 – corporate dwelling place (shekinah) unity of the brethren is like the oil upon the head running down the Body as the dew of the Mount of Transfiguration and the dew that descended upon the mountains of Zion where the High Priest of Zion – Wisdom – serves in the Temple of Zion.] *My locks with the drops of the night. The Shulamite - I have taken off My robe* [to relax] *How can I put it on again? I have washed My feet* [to put My feet up]*; How can I defile them? My Beloved put His hand by the latch of the door, and my heart yearned for Him" (Song of Solomon 5.1-4* NKJV *comments in brackets mine).*

TOTAL EASE – UTTER RELAXATION – PERFECT ABSOLUTE REST. Recall from our MEL GEL #2 Class entitled "Shekinah Sabbath" that myrrh oil is the sacrament (visible sign) of *theosis* – the transformation of a human being back into a divine being made in God's image. *"I have come to My garden, My sister, My spouse; I have gathered My myrrh" (SS 5.1).* The perfumed myrrh oil was kept in the Holy of Holies. *"But the dove found no REST for the sole of her foot, and she returned unto him into the ark" (Genesis 8.9a).*

"The LORD shall send the rod of your strength out of Zion [place where Wisdom – Bride of Christ – ministers]. *Rule in the midst of Your enemies! Your people shall be volunteers in the day of Your power; in the beauty of holiness, from the womb* (matrix) *of the morning, you have the dew of Your youth [resurrection life and the restoration of longevity]. The LORD has sworn and will not relent, 'You are a priest forever according to the Order of Melchizedek'" (Psalms 110.2-4* NKJV*).*

Lamsa's Aramaic version says: *"² The LORD will send forth the scepter of His power out of Zion, and He will rule over thine enemies* [His Queen rules with the King]. *³ Thy people shall be glorious in the day of Thy power; arrayed in the beauty of holiness from the womb, I have begotten thee as a child from the ages.* [Recall from MEL GEL #2 that when a royal high priest was anointed with the myrrh oil, it made him a Child of Wisdom – the Son of God (Melchizedek is made like unto the Son of God – Hebrews 7.3) – who was perfumed with oil from the Tree of Life] *⁴ The LORD has sworn and will not lie, You are a priest for ever after the Order of Melchizedek."*

The *Dead Sea Scrolls* relates *"The Songs of the Sabbath Sacrifice"* to Melchizedek who is called the chief angelic (cherubic) priest in one fragment. These *Sabbath Songs* focus on God as King and are heavenly focused.

The community that recites the *Sabbath Songs* is led through a progressive experience. It's a corporate 13-week cycle.

Nitzan's *Qumran Prayer and Religious Poetry* speaks of "a gradual ascent in the status of those engaged in praise, reaching its peak in the songs portraying the angelic priesthood, the divine throne and chariot." The mysteries of the angelic priesthood are described as an ecstatic celebration of the sabbatical number seven, producing a climax at the center of the work.

The community brings the Sabbath Songs alive by giving spirit to the heavenly temple until the worshippers experience the holiness of the *Merkabah* (God's Chariot

Throne) and the Sabbath Sacrifice conducted by the angelic High Priests. The intense preoccupation with angelic priests suggests that the Sabbath Songs are related to the glorification of the Melchizedek Priesthood.

Since these Sabbath Songs are said to invoke angelic praise and describe Sabbath worship of the angelic priesthood in the heavenly temple, the *Songs of the Sabbath Sacrifices* are also known as the Angelic Liturgy. These Sabbath Songs provide a virtual experience of worship in the heavenly temple. This includes both heavenly and earthly communities participating in heavenly worship with a parallel between the angelic and human priestly service. In *Jubilees 31.14,* Isaac stresses the parallel between angelic and human priestly service when he blesses Levi: *"May [God] draw you and your seed near to Him from all flesh TO SERVE IN HIS SANCTUARY AS THE ANGELS OF THE PRESENCE AND THE HOLY ONES."*

Angelic praise around the Throne of God with Is-real's praise joining the angels originally went up only on the Sabbath and certain holidays. There's a very close connection between heavenly and earthly worshippers.

NOTE: The composition of the Angelic Liturgy (i.e., *The Songs of the Sabbath Sacrifices*) is preserved in ten sections of the Dead Sea Scrolls: eight sections come from Qumran Cave 4 (4Q400-4Q407), one from Qumran Cave 11 (11Q17) and one from Masada (Mas1k).

According to Carol Newsom in her book *He Has Established for Himself Priests: Human and Angelic Priesthood in the Qumran Sabbath Shirot* [p. 113-118], the Sabbath Songs were used by the Qumran Community, who themselves insisted that they alone preserved the true and faithful priesthood. Even though the Qumran Priesthood did not do their sacrificial service at Jerusalem's Temple (second corrupted temple was Herod's Temple), their recitation of the Sabbath Song cultivated the sense of the Presence of the Living God in the heavenly temple.

Margaret Barker speaks of the Qumran Community in her book, *"Temple Theology"* [p. 22-24]: The Qumran Community claimed to be the true priests of God. [Therefore] Their devout hearts kept meticulous track of what a true priest of God was... angelic priests. The angels ascending and descending on the Son of Man in John 1:51 were both angelic messengers and human messengers who stood before the Throne of the Holy One and have been born in the Holy of Holies. These are the ones who have entered the Kingdom of God (John 3.5) and have been commissioned into the Order of Melchizedek who are "equal to angels and are sons of God, being sons of the resurrection" (Luke 20.36). Resurrection life for the sons of God on earth [kings and priests of the Order of Melchizedek] is a *theosis* – a transformation of a human being back into our original created state – a divine being made in the image of God (Genesis 1.27). We need to shift our RESURRECTION MINDSETS from a post-mortem experience to a living and active transformation of God's

47

people into the angelic state. Enoch models this reality. He was transformed into an angel (2 Enoch 22), resurrected, and then sent back to earth. This is our journey back to the future where we are gradually transformed into the very image of God.

Although much of the text of *The Songs of the Sabbath* is lost (fragments), I believe that what remains has a message for us in this Kingdom Day. The only standard elements in each song is the heading "Song of the Sabbath Sacrifice" and the call to praise, which introduces the body of the Song.

The 13 Songs of the Sabbath Sacrifice can be separated into three sections:

[1] Songs 1-5,

[2] Songs 6-8, and

[3] Songs 9-13.

Let's visualize the Thirteen Songs as a pyramidal structure where the Seventh Song serves as the climax:

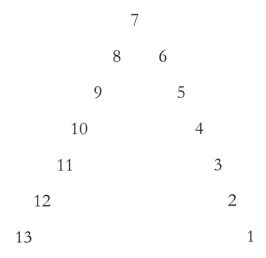

SONGS 1-5 describe the establishment of the angelic priesthood and its duties, as well as describing the praise of heavenly priests. The only references to the human priesthood and worshippers are in the first two Sabbath Songs.

SONGS 6-8 have repetitious literary structure where the number "7" figures prominently. The sixth and eighth Sabbath Songs contain the praises and blessings uttered by angels designated as the "seven chief princes." The central and Seventh Sabbath Song describes the way that the heavenly temple itself bursts into praise, and concludes with a description of the inner room (Holy of Holies) and the chariot throne of God.

<u>SONGS 9-13</u> have a progressive description of the heavenly temple and its praises culminates in a description of the *merkabah* and the angelic high priests in the twelfth and thirteen songs. It begins in the Ninth Sabbath Song with the outer temple, then moves to a description of the veil in the Tenth Sabbath Song. The veil separates the outer area from the inner room (Holy of Holies). The Eleventh Sabbath Song describes the Inner Shrine (Holy of Holies), concluding with an account of multiple chariot thrones that praise God. The Twelfth Sabbath Song extends the description of the *Merkabah,* which bear the Glory with an account of the praises of angels who go in and out of the heavenly temple. The Thirteenth Sabbath Song gives the account of the priestly angels and their sacrificial service.

The Sabbath Songs restrict the presence of God (glory of God) imagery to the appearance of a human-like figure to the chariot (i.e., *merkabah*) and its features (without human-like figures above the firmament).

HEAVENLY HIGH PRIESTHOOD or ETERNAL HIGH PRIESTHOOD - *The Dead Sea Scrolls* identify Melchizedek as one of the *Elohim* (sons of God), and specifies that Melchizedek's role is priestly:

DEAD SEA SCROLLS

The Coming of Melchizedek

11 Q13 2.4-11

4 [the interpretation] is that it applies [to the L]ast Days and concerns the captives, just as [Isaiah said: "To proclaim the jubilee to the captives" (Isaiah 61.1) ...] and 5 whose teachers have been hidden and kept secr[et], even from the inheritance of Melchizedek, f[or ...] and they are the inherit[ance of Melchize]dek, who 6 will return them to what is rightfully theirs. He will proclaim to them the jubilee, thereby releasing th[em from the debt of a]ll their sin. This word [will thus co]me 7 in the first week of the jubilee period that follows ni[ne j]ubilee periods, 8 when he shall atone for all the SONS OF [LIGHT] and the people[e who are pre]destined to Mel[chi]zedek. [...] upo[n the]m [...] For 9 this is the time decreed for "the year of Melchiz[edek]'s favor" (Isaiah 61.2, modified) and for [his] hos[ts, together] with the holy ones of God, for a kingdom of judgment, just as it is written 10 concerning him in the Songs of David. "A GODLIKE BEING has taken his place in the coun[cil of God;] in the midst of the divine beings he holds judgment (Ps 82.1). Scripture also s[ays] about him. "Over [it] 11 take your seat in the highest heaven; a DIVINE BEING will judge the peoples" (Psalms 7.7-8).

The terms "Godlike Beings" and "Divine Beings" are used continually in the *Dead Sea Scrolls*. By the way, I used these books for my Melchizedek Songs of the Sabbath Sacrifice Study:

> [1] *"The Dead Sea Scrolls – Charlesworth – Hebrew, Aramaic, and Greek Texts with English Translations – Angelic Liturgy: Songs of the Sabbath Sacrifice"* ISBN 3-16-146914-3 from The Princeton Theological Seminary Dead Sea Scrolls project

> [2] *"A New Translation THE DEAD SEA SCROLLS"* by Michael O. Wise, Martin G. Abegg Jr., Edward M. Cook, 101. The Songs of the Sabbath Sacrifice"

In MEL GEL #2, we spoke about a Melchizedek Company of a congregation of the Sons of Righteousness that "stand in the council of God." It's spoken of in *Psalm 82.1 – "A godlike being* [mature sons who are "living creatures" made after the Order of Melchizedek who together make up a feminine Living Creature – the Bride of Christ] *has taken his place in the council of God in the midst of the divine beings he holds judgment."*

The concept of "Godlike Divine Beings" is a theme throughout *The Songs of the Sabbath Sacrifice*:

- GODLIKE BEINGS of all the Most Holy Ones ... in divinity among the eternally holy... have become for Him priests... ministers of the

Presence in His glorious inner room. [Portion from the song for the first Sabbath – 4Q400 Frag. 1, Col. 1, vs. 2-4]

- In the congregation of all the DIVINE BEINGS of GODLIKE BEINGS, He inscribed His statutes with respect to all the works of the Spirit and precepts of …knowledge, people of discernment glorified by God who draw near to knowledge… [Portion from the song for the first Sabbath – 4Q400 Frag, 1, Col. 1, vs. 4-5]

- Priests of the inner sanctum who serve before the King of Holiness, He established them for Himself as the holy ones of the Holy of Holies. The *Merkabah (rbw)* is among them according to the assembly […] from knowledge. [Portion from the song for the first Sabbath – 4Q400 Frag. 1, Col. 1, vs. 8,10,11]

- They do not tolerate any who pervert the way. And there is nothing unclean in their holy places (i.e., souls). [Portion from the song for the first Sabbath – 4Q400 Frag. 1, Col. 1, vs. 14]

- God of DIVINE BEINGS who are priests of the highest heights. They are who draw near, priests of the inner sanctum. [Portion from the song for the first Sabbath – 4Q400 Frag. 1, Col. 1, vs. 19-20]

- The King of the DIVINE BEINGS who inhabit the seven holy temples. [Portion from the song for the first Sabbath – 4Q400 Frag. 1, Col. 2, vs. 7]

- His glory is in the council of the GODLIKE BEINGS. [Portion from the song for the first Sabbath – 4Q400 Frag. 1, Col. 2, vs. 9]

- Praise Your glory among the wise DIVINE BEINGS who are utterly holy extolling Your Kingdom. They are honored in all the camps of the GODLIKE BEINGS and feared by those who direct human affairs. [Portion from the song for the second Sabbath – 4Q400 Frag. 2, vs. 1-2]

- Beyond other DIVINE BEINGS and humans alike. They tell of His royal splendor as they truly know it, and exalt His glory in all the heavens of His rule. [Portion from the song for the second Sabbath – 4Q400 Frag. 2, vs. 3-4]

- [They sing] wonderful psalms according to [their insight] throughout the highest heaven, and declare [the surpassing] glory of the King of the GODLIKE BEINGS in the stations of their habitation. [Portion from the song for the second Sabbath – 4Q400 Frag. 2, vs. 4-5]

- The war of the GODLIKE BEINGS... the weapons of warfare belong to the God of DIVINE BEINGS... the armies of heaven and wonders of all the DIVINE SPIRITS shall run at His command… armies of DIVINE SPIRITS at wars in the clouds, but the victory shall belong to the God of DIVINE BEINGS. [Portion from the song for the fifth Sabbath – 4Q402, Frags. 3-4, vs. 7-10]

- To the King of the [wise] GODLIKE BEINGS belong all matters of knowledge; indeed, the God of Knowledge causes all that happens forever. Through His knowledge and by means of His glorious plan all the eternal seasons have come to be… He has created the former things at their times, and the latter things… at the time appointed for them. None among those who are knowledgeable – those to whom revelation has come – can grasp these things before He does them; even when He brings them into existence, none can truly comprehend them. None of the DIVINE BEINGS. [Portion from the song for the fifth Sabbath – 4Q402, Frags. 3-4, vs. 12-14]

Scripture tells us that we are renewed in knowledge unto the knowledge of the Son of God unto a perfect man: *"Lie not one to another, seeing that you have put off the old man with his deeds; And have PUT ON THE NEW MAN, WHICH IS RENEWED IN KNOWLEDGE AFTER THE IMAGE OF HIM THAT CREATED HIM" (Colossians 3.9-10 KJV)*. We are told in Ephesians 4 that the five-fold ministry gifts (apostles, prophets, evangelists, pastors and teachers) were given *"for the perfecting of the saints, for the work of ministry, for the edifying of the Body of Christ: UNTIL WE ALL COME in the unity of the faith, and OF KNOWLEDGE OF THE SON OF GOD, UNTO A PERFECT MAN, unto the measure of the stature of the fullness of Christ"* (Ephesians 4.12-13).

In the Name of His Holiness the seventh chief prince blesses all the holy who establish knowledge [Portion from the song for the sixth Sabbath - Mas1k Frag. 2, vs. 3.23-24]

- Knowledge of the eternal GODLIKE BEINGS [Portion from the song for the sixth Sabbath – Mas1k Frag. 1, vs. 11]

- All the DIVINE BEINGS who are appointed for righteousness [Portion from the song for the sixth Sabbath – Mas1K Frag. 2, vs. 5]

- The Warrior is over all the GODLIKE BEINGS [Portion from the song for the sixth Sabbath – Mas1k Frag. 2, vs. 6.2]

- All the DIVINE BEINGS are wise in His Truth. (Remember our study of the Sabbath Rest, in Hebrews chapter 4.)

- The warrior deeds of the DIVINE BEINGS are insightful. His warrior power will bless all who are perfect in The Way that they might continue forever in the company of all the ETERNAL BEINGS. He will bless all who wait for Him that His compassionate loving-kindness might return to them.

- Those who are holy among the GODLIKE sanctify the glorious King and He sanctifies the princes of praise by His holiness [circular]

- [All you] wise [spirits] of light; together laud the utterly brilliant firmament that girds [His] holy temple. Praise Him, GODLIKE SPIRITS, laud[ing] eternally the firmament of the uttermost heaven, all [its be]ams and walls, all its structure and crafted desi[gn.] The utterly holy spirits, living divinities, eternally holy spirits above all the hol[y ones …] wondrous and wonderful, majesty and splendor and marvel. Glory abides in the perfected light of knowledge [Portion from the song for the seventh Sabbath – 4Q403 Frag. 1, Col. 1 (with Mas1k Frag. 2, 4Q404 Frags. 1-2 and 4Q405 Frag. 3, Col. 2, vs. 42-45]

- The likeness of LIVING DIVINE BEINGS is carved on the walls of the vestibules by which the King enters. [The Living Creature's kingdom within]. They are luminous spiritual figures in the innermost sanctums of the King... figures of glorious light... wondrous spirits. [Portion from the song for the ninth Sabbath – 4Q405 Frags. 14-15, Col. 1, vs. 5]

- In the midst of the glorious spirits stand wondrous embroidered works – figures of LIVING DIVINE BEINGS – in the glorious innermost sanctums that belong to the structure of the utterly holy temple in the innermost sanctums of the King. [Portion from the song for the ninth Sabbath – 4Q405 Frags. 14-15, Col. 1, vs. 6-7]

- The spirits of the perpetual DIVINE BEINGS are the figures of the innermost sanctuary of the King. They are the spiritual handiwork of the wondrous firmament made utterly pure. [Portion from the song for the eleventh Sabbath – 4Q405 Frags. 19 a-d (with 11Q17 Frags. 12-15), vs. 3-4]

- The luminous forms of the LIVING GODLIKE BEINGS are spiritual forms... spirits of knowledge, truth, and righteousness in the Holy of Holies. [Portion from the song for the eleventh Sabbath – 4Q405 Frags. 19 a-d (with 11Q17 Frags. 12-15), vs. 4]

- All the holy handiworks of living GODLIKE BEINGS are wondrously connected to each other. Embroidered spirits (figures of the GODLIKE BEINGS) are engraved all around the glorious bricks. These are glorious figures. They are the handiwork belonging to the splendid and majestic bricks. All these handiworks are living GODLIKE BEINGS, and their figures are holy angels. [Portion from the song for the eleventh Sabbath – 4Q405 Frags. 19 a-d (with 11Q17 Frags. 12-15), vs. 5-6]

- From beneath the marvelous innermost sanctums is heard the quiet voice of GODLIKE BEINGS praising. [Portion from the song for the eleventh Sabbath – 4Q405 Frags. 19 a-d (with 11Q17 Frags. 12-15), vs. 3-4]

- GODLIKE SPIRITS of purity and holiness are steadfast in serving and have a seat similar to His royal throne in His glorious innermost sanctums – His glorious chariots, holy cherubim, luminous wheel-beings. [Portion from the song for the eleventh Sabbath – 4Q405 Frags. 20, Col. 2 + Frags. 21-22 (with 11Q17 Frags. 3-6), vs. 2-3]

- The spirits of the LIVING GODLIKE BEINGS perpetually move to and fro following the glory of the wondrous chariots. The Cherubim bless the image of the Chariot-Throne that appears above the firmament. The Cherubim fall before Him and bless Him; as they arise, the quiet voice of God is heard, which is followed by a tumult of joyous praise. As they unfold their wings, God's quiet voice is heard again. After the Cherubim bless the image of Chariot-Throne, they joyously proclaim (acclaim) the splendor of the luminous firmament that spread beneath His glorious seat. [Portion from the song for the twelfth Sabbath – 4Q405 Frags. 20, Col. 2 + Frags. 21-22 (with 11Q17 Frags. 3-6), vs. 7-9]

- The GODLIKE BEINGS are fearful and powerful. All their utterly wondrous acts by the power of God. They exalt the warrior acts of God from the four foundations of the wondrous firmament. [Portion from the song for the twelfth Sabbath – 11Q17 Frags. 5-6, vs. 3-4]

- The wondrous GODLIKE BEINGS shall not be shaken. They remain steadfast in every task. [Portion from the song for the twelfth Sabbath – 4Q405 Frags. 23, Col. 1, vs. 4-5]

- The GODLIKE BEINGS are in charge of His whole offering. [Portion from the song for the twelfth Sabbath – 4Q405 Frags. 23, Col. 1, vs. 5]

- The GODLIKE BEINGS praise Him when they first take their positions while all the spirits of the splendid firmaments continuously rejoice in His glory. A voice of blessing comes from all of His divisions telling of His glorious firmaments, and His gates praise with a joyful noise. [Portion from the song for the twelfth Sabbath – 4Q405 Frags.

23, Col. 1, vs. 6-8]

- When the wise DIVINE BEINGS enter through glorious portals, and when the holy angels go forth to their realms, the portals through which they enter and the gates through which they exit declare the glory of the King. They bless and praise all the GODLIKE SPIRITS each time they exit or enter through the holy gates. None of them fails to acknowledge anything. They neither run from The Way nor reverence anything not a part of it. [Portion from the song for the twelfth Sabbath – 4Q405 Frags. 23, Col. 1, vs. 8-11]

- Awesome fear of the King grips all the GODLIKE BEINGS when He sends them forth. [Portion from the song for the twelfth Sabbath – 4Q405 Frags. 23, Col. 1, vs. 13]

Yeshua Ha Machiach (Jesus Christ) is the only High Priest of the Order of Melchizedek (Hebrews 2.17; 4.14-15; 5.1,5,10; 6.20; 7.26; 8.1; 9.11; 10.21

Hebrews 4 Lamsa's Aramaic [my comments in brackets]

1 Let us therefore fear, while the PROMISE OF ENTERING INTO HIS REST REMAINS, *lest some amongst you find they are prevented from entering.*

2 For THE GOSPEL *was preached to us as it was to them also, but* THE WORD *they* heard *did not benefit them, because it was not mixed with* faith *in those who heard it.*

3 But WE WHO HAVE BELIEVED WILL ENTER INTO REST, *as He said, As I have sworn in my wrath, they shall not enter into my* REST; *for* BEHOLD, THE WORKS OF GOD WERE FROM THE VERY FOUNDATION OF THE WORLD.

4 For he said CONCERNING THE SABBATH, GOD RESTED ON THE SEVENTH DAY FROM ALL HIS WORKS.

5 And here again he said, They shall not enter into my rest,

6 There was a chance for some to enter therein, but they TO WHOM THE GOSPEL *WAS FIRST PREACHED DID NOT ENTER BECAUSE THEY WOULD NOT LISTEN;*

7 And again, after a long time he appointed another day, AS IT IS WRITTEN above; for DAVID SAID, TODAY IF YOU HEAR HIS VOICE, HARDEN NOT YOUR HEARTS, [My comment – King David is passing the baton to run after the Order of Melchizedek that has been ordained since the beginning of time. Behold, a New Kingdom Age with the banner of the Order of Melchizedek is here. The "ages to come" is now!!! Three ancient stars – Paul the Apostle, King David, and Melchizedek – are connected to one another, and are imparting gemstone prisms in this hour for the restoration of our world(s) back to its original design. The Melchizedek Army is marching. The Army of Melchizedek is getting out their rods to rule in Christ.]

Hebrews 4 Lamsa's Aramaic [my comments in brackets] (continued)

8 For if Joshua the son of Nun had given them REST, *he would not afterward have spoken of another day.*

9 IT IS THEREFORE THE DUTY OF THE PEOPLE OF GOD TO KEEP THE SABBATH.

10 For HE WHO HAS ENTERED INTO HIS REST ALSO HAS CEASED FROM HIS OWN WORKS, AS GOD DID FROM HIS.

11 LET US STRIVE THEREFORE TO ENTER INTO THE REST, lest any man fall like those who were disobedient.

[The word "**strive**" is the Greek word *spoudazo* (pronounced spoo-dad-zo). It carries the meaning to make haste, to endeavor, to exert oneself, to be diligent, labor, study, be prompt and earnest.

The word "**enter**" is the Greek word *eiserchomai* (pronounced ce-er'-khom-ahee) - to enter, to arise, come into existence, begin to be, to come into life]

Hebrews 4 Lamsa's Aramaic [my comments in brackets] (continued)

12 For THE WORD OF GOD IS LIVING AND POWERFUL AND SHARPER THAN ANY TWO-EDGED SWORD, piercing even to the point of division between soul and spirit, and between the joints and marrow and bones, and is a discerner of the thoughts and intents of the heart. ["the gospel" in verse 2 is connected to "the Word of God" in verse 12]

13 And there is no creature hidden from His sight; but all things

KINGDOM SECRETS are revealed to those who access His throne (Hebrews 4.16). See Daniel 2.21-22; Proverbs 3.32; Psalm 25.14. In the secret place, there the Father is and He sees the secret things (Matthew 6.3-6, 17-21). In the secret place, NOTHING (which is in secret) will manifest the things that the Father is doing through Christ in you, the hope of glory - crucified, buried and risen - the Word made flesh dwelling among us. This Word that in the beginning was and continues to be… continues to uphold all things by its power, even the dust of our earth.

Can't help but incorporate the Hebrew Living Letters here! Did you know that the Hebrew Living Letters and the Blood of the Lamb slain before the foundation of the world are the protoplasm of creation? *"In the beginning was the Word, and the Word was with God, and the Word was God" (John 1.1).* The Word is made up of letters. The letters -- these individual spiritual forces (energetic forces) – inherent in Christ were birthed from His essential, intrinsic essence, which was originally included wholly in the Word. The first born of all creation is the very thing that constitutes every living substance. It is the protoplasm of the universe. It is the individual spiritual forces that originally belonged, and still belong, to the nature of Christ. The first born of all creation is the letters of the Word – the Hebrew Alphabet, i.e., The Hebrew Living Letters. Therefore, when the Hebrew mystics say that the letters of the Hebrew Alphabet were created first of all out of nothing but God's desire – His divine will - they are saying the Hebrew Living Letters are at a foundational quantum level of all created things.

Hebrews 4 Lamsa's Aramaic [my comments in brackets] (continued)

14 We have, therefore, a GREAT HIGH PRIEST WHO HAS ASCENDED INTO HEAVEN, JESUS CHRIST, THE SON OF GOD; let us remain firm in His faith.

15 For we do not have a High Priest who cannot share our infirmities, but we have one who was tempted with everything as we are, and yet without sin.

16 Let us, therefore, come openly to the Throne of His Grace, that we may obtain mercy and find grace to help in time in need.

4 – SEVEN CHIEF PRINCES OF HIGHEST PRAISE

The term "angelic" appears to be so much more than we have previously understood or have been taught.

Question: What do you think of when I say the word "angelic"?

Answer: Angels. Right? Or could it be something more?

Turn your discernment on and please allow me to expand your horizons. So far I have seen angels themselves, the Seven Spirits of God, High Priests going into the Holy of Holies, and humans made divine again being referred to as "angelic." Notice that they are all living beings.

Let's review some points that we went over in our last MEL GEL Class called "Sabbath Sacrifices and Absolute Rest" before we get into the Seven Chief Princes of Highest Praise:

Recall how the community that recited the Angelic Liturgy (i.e., *The Songs of the Sabbath Sacrifices*) was led through a progressive experience for 13 weeks where those engaged in this highest praise participated in an ecstatic celebration. Remember, in context, *The Songs of the Sabbath Sacrifices* were used by the Qumran Community who insisted that they were the true priests of God. Their devout hearts kept meticulous track of what a true priest of God was… angelic priests. The angels ascending and descending on the Son of Man in John 1.51 were both angelic messengers and human messengers who stood before the Throne of the Holy One and have been born in the Holy of Holies. In *Jubilees 31.14*, Isaac blessed Levi: *"May [God] draw you and your seed near to Him from all flesh to serve in His sanctuary as the angels of the presence and the holy ones."*

We have much to learn from that community that brought the Sabbath Songs alive by giving spirit to the heavenly temple until the worshippers experienced the holiness of the *Merkabah* (God's Chariot Throne) and the Sabbath Sacrifice was conducted by the angelic High Priests. Remember that the intense preoccupation with angelic priests suggests that *The Songs of the Sabbath Sacrifices* (i.e., Sabbath Songs) are related to the glorification of the Melchizedek Priesthood.

Since these Sabbath Songs are said to invoke angelic praise and describe Sabbath worship of the angelic priesthood in the heavenly temple, *The Songs of the Sabbath Sacrifices* are also known as the Angelic Liturgy.

These Sabbath Songs provide a virtual experience of worship in the heavenly temple. This includes both heavenly and earthly communities participating in heavenly worship. The *Dead Sea Scrolls* relates *"The Songs of the Sabbath Sacrifice"* to Melchizedek who is called the chief angelic (cherubic) priest in one fragment.

Although much of the text of *The Songs of the Sabbath* is lost (fragments), I believe that what remains has a message for us in this Kingdom Day.

The Thirteen Songs of the Sabbath Sacrifice can be separated into three sections and can be visualized as pyramidal structure where the Seventh Song serves as the climax:

[1] Songs 1-5,

[2] Songs 6-8, and

[3] Songs 9-13.

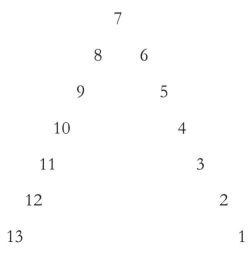

We, as a contingent of the Heavenly High Priesthood (i.e., Eternal or Perpetual High Priesthood made after the Order of Melchizedek), will be zeroing in on the center section: Songs 6-8, where the number "7" figures prominently. The Sixth and Eighth Songs contain the praises and blessings uttered by "seven chief princes." The central and Seventh Song describes the way that the heavenly temple itself bursts into praise, and concludes with a description of the inner room (Holy of Holies) and the chariot throne of God.

Let's break this all down. Princes are learning to crown Him as King. When you become a king, Yeshua becomes King of Kings. Our Pattern Son – Messiah Yeshua (Jesus Christ)'s soul was filled with the Seven Spirits of God. *"And there shall come forth a shoot out of the stem of Jesse, and a branch shall grow out of his roots; and he shall be at peace, and the Spirit of the Lord shall rest upon him, the Spirit of Wisdom and Understanding, the Spirit of Counsel and Might, the Spirit of Knowledge and of the Reverence of the Lord"* (Isaiah 11.1-2 *Aramaic*).

The Seven Spirits of God are also our governors and tutors until we fully become a Mature Son (of Full Age). *Galatians 4.1-2* says: *"Now I say, that the heir, as long as he is a child, differs nothing from a servant, though he be lord of all; but is under TUTORS AND GOVERNORS UNTIL the time appointed of the Father."*

Please keep in mind the Seven Spirit of God when I am speaking about the Seven Chief Princes said to be angelic. In one dimension, these seven living beings/forces (Seven Spirits of God) divided by the 22 Hebrew Living Letters, which are the essence of the Word of God, are part of the circle (or compass) the LORD has set upon the face of your depths (Proverbs 8.27).

The key is to press-in to take on maturity, which literally is to believe for the possession of your own soul with the same Seven Spirits of God that possessed Yeshua's soul (Hebrews 10.39).

Keeping the Seven Spirits of God in mind, let's consider that during the 13-week "Songs of the Sabbath Sacrifice" cycle, the song for the sixth Sabbath has each of the seven chief princes recite a psalm; then each of the same seven beings offers a blessing.

Seven Chief Princes Each Recite a Psalm:

[1] FIRST CHIEF PRINCE – 7 WONDROUS BLESSINGS - A psalm of blessing will be spoken in the language of the first chief prince to the Eternal God, which incorporates his language's seven wondrous blessings. Then he will bless the K[ing of all the eternally holy seven times with seven] [wondrous words of blessing.] ~ *Mas1k Frag 2, 1-3*

71

[2] SECOND CHIEF PRINCE - 7 WONDROUS EXALTATIONS - A psalm of exaltation will be spoken in the language of the second chief prince to the King of truth and [righteousness, incorporating his language's seven wondrous exaltations. Then he will magnify the God] of all the div[ine beings who are appointed for righteousness seven times with seven words of [wondrous] exaltation. ~ *Mas1k Frag 2, 3-6*

[3] THIRD CHIEF PRINCE - 7 WONDROUS GLORIFICATIONS - A psalm of glorification will be spoken in the language of the third chief prince, a glorification of His faithfulness directed to the King of the angels, incorporating his language's seven wondrous glorifications. Then he will glorify the God of the exalted angels seven times with seven words of wondrous glorification. ~ *Mas1k Frag 2, 6-6.1*

[4] FOURTH CHIEF PRINCE - 7 WONDROUS WARRIOR UTTERANCES - A psalm of praise will be spoken in the language of the fourth chief prince to the Warrior who is over all the godlike beings, incorporating his language's seven wondrous warrior utterances. Then he will praise the God of warrior power seven times with seve[n] words of [wondrous] pra[ise.] ~ *Mas1k Frag 2, 6.2-6.3*

[5] FIFTH CHIEF PRINCE - 7 WONDROUS
THANKSGIVINGS - A psalm of thanksgiving will be
spoken in the language of the fifth chief prince to the
glorious [K]in[g], incorporating his language's seven
wondrous tha[nk]sgivings. Then he will thank the
glorified God seven times [with sev]en [wo]rds of
wondrous thanksgiving. ~ *Mas1k Frag 2, 6.3-6.4*

[6] SIXTH CHIEF PRINCE - 7 WONDROUS
REJOICINGS – [A psa]lm of rejoicing will be spoken
in the language of the sixth chief prince to the God of
goodness, incorporating his language's seven cries of
[wondrous] rejoicing. Then he will cry out with
rejoicing to the King of goodness, seven times with
s[even words of] wondrous rejoicing. ~ *Mas1k Frag 2,
6.4-6.5*

[7] SEVENTH CHIEF PRINCE – A psalm of musical
praise will be spoken in the language of the seventh
[chief] pri[nce], a powerful musical praise to the God of
holiness incorporating his language's seven wond[erful
praise elements.] Then he will sing praise to the King of
holiness seven times with [seven] wondrous words of
musical [praise,] together with seven psalms of blessing
to Him, seven psalms of exaltation of His
righteousness, seven psalms of glorifications of His
Kingdom, seven psalms of pra[ise of His glory,] seven
psalms of thanksgiving for His wondrous doings, seven
psa[lms of re]joicing for His might and seven psalms of
musical praise of His holiness. The generations of [...]

seven times with seven wondrous words, words of [...] ~ *Mas1k Frag 2, 6.6-6.9*

NOTICE the repetitive "seven times with seven words" for each of the 7 chief princes. Then...

7 Chief Princes Blessings:

[1] FIRST CHIEF PRINCE – In the name of the glory of God [the first of] the ch[ief] princes [*my addition - The Spirit of the Lord*] [will bl]ess [all the... and all] the wise [with seven] wondrous [w]ords, blessing all th[ei]r councils in [His Holy] Temple [with se]ven wondr[ous] wo[r]ds, [and ble]ssing those who know eternal things. ~ *Mas1k Frag 2, 6.10-6.11*

[2] SECOND CHIEF PRINCE – [In the name of] His Truth [the second] [chief prince [*my addition - The Spirit of the Wisdom*] will bless] all [their] stati[on with] sev[en] wondrous words. Indeed, he shall bless with seven [marvelous] words. [He will also bless all who exalt the] King with seven words of His marvelous glory, and he will bless all who are eternally pure. ~ *Mas1k Frag 2, 6.11-6.13*

[3] THIRD CHIEF PRINCE – [In the name of] His exalted kingdom the th[ird of the chief prince [*my addition - The Spirit of Understanding*] will bless] all who are exalted in knowledge with seven words of exaltation, blessing all [the divine beings] wise [in His

Truth.] Indeed, he shall bless with seven marvelous words. He will also bless all those [appointed for] righteousness with sev[en] marvelous [w]ords. ~ *Mas1k Frag 2, 6.14-6.16*

[4] FOURTH CHIEF PRINCE – In the name of the majes[tic Ki]ng [the fourth] of the chief prince [*my addition - The Spirit of Counsel*] will bless all who wal[k upri]ght with [sev]en maj[estic] words. He will also bless those who establish majesty with seven [wondrous w]ords, blessing all the divine beings [who draw] near to [His] verit[able] truth with seven righteous words, so that they can gain [His glor]ious compassion. ~ *Mas1k Frag 2, 6.16-6.18*

[5] FIFTH CHIEF PRINCE – In the name of His [majestic] wonders [*my addition – the fifth*] chief prince [*my addition - the Spirit of Might/Power*] will bless all who comprehend the mysteries of pure [insight] with seven w[ords] of [His] exalted truth. [He will also bless] all who are quick to do His will with seven [wondrous words] blessing those who confess Him with seven majestic [wo]rds comprising a wondrous thanksgiving. ~ *Mas1k Frag 2, 6.18-6.21*

[6] SIXTH CHIEF PRINCE – In the name of the warrior deeds of the divine beings the sixth chief prince will bless all who are insightful warriors with seven wondrous words of His warrior power. He will also bless all who are PERFECT in the way with seven wondrous words, that they might continue forever in

the company of all the [eter]nal beings [*my comment - divine cherubic form*]. Yet again will he bless all who wait for Him with seven wondrous words, that His compassionate loving-kindness might return to them. ~ *Mas1k Frag 2, 6.21-6.23*

[7] SEVENTH CHIEF PRINCE – In the name of His Holiness the [sev]enth chief prince [*my addition - the Spirit of the Fear of the Lord*] will bless all the holy who establish knowledge with seven words of [His] wondrous holiness. He will also bless all who exalt His laws with se[ven] wondrous [wo]rds that act as mighty shields. Yet again will he bless all who are prede[stined] for righteous[ness], they who praise His glorious kingdom [forever and] ever, with seven wondrous words that lead to eternal peace. ~ *Mas1k Frag 2, 6.23-6.26*

"Then in the [name of His holiness] all the [chief] princes [will bless in unis]on the God of divine beings with all [their] sevenfold appointed words of blessing. They will also bless those predestined for righteousness and all those blessed of [...] the eternally [bless]ed [...] to them, saying, "Blessed be [the] Lord, the Kin[g of] all, exalted above every blessing and pr[aise, He who blesses all the hol]y who bless [Him] and those [who declare His righteous]ness in the name of His glory, [He who] blesses all who receive blessings, forever. ~ *Dead Sea Scroll, Mas1k Frag 2, 6.26-29*

Angelic Priests Tidbits

- Eternal godlike beings who know eternal things.

- Divine beings appointed for righteousness.

- Extol God's Kingdom among the utterly holy and His glory among the wise divine beings.

- Priests of the highest heights who draw near.

- Priests of the inner sanctum – the most holy ones – serve the King of Holiness.

- Minister of the Presence in His glorious inner room.

- People of discernment gloried of God.

- In the congregation of all the divine beings of godlike beings, He inscribed His statutes with respect to all works of the spirit and precepts of knowledge.

- The *Merkabah* is among them according to the assembly.

Before this class, Ann Ritter mentioned: "On 22 speaking about '7.' " Perhaps she knows how profound it is that on September 22, 2016 (today) we are speaking about the Seven Chief Princes of Highest Praise.

In the language of math, the light in God's Temple speaks of His eternal never-ending light. The pattern of the Temple Menorah (Golden Candlestick) include 7 lamps with 22 almonds in various stages of life. Divide 7 into 22 and you get 3.14 - Pi. Pi is a number so close to infinity that it appears to go on forever. Pi is the main feature of a circle, because the circumference of a circle is its diameter multiplied by PI. Behold, the Lamp in God's Temple contains a picture of a mysterious engraving of a *"circle upon the face of the deep" (Proverbs 8.27)*. Please refer to our first MEL GEL Class – *The Restoration of All Things and The Engravings.*

Let's look closer at this illuminating circle upon the face of the deep for our little world here on earth. The Temple Menorah has seven branches or seven lamps. Scripture connects seven lamps of fire burning before the throne to the Seven Spirits of God:

"¹ After these things [revelation of the seven churches] *I looked and behold, a door was open in heaven; and the first voice which I heard was like a trumpet talking with me, which said, Come up here and I will show you things which must come to pass. ² And immediately I was in the spirit; and behold, a throne was set in heaven, and one sat on the throne. ³ And He who sat resembled a stone of jasper and sardonyx, and round about the throne was a rainbow resembling emeralds. ⁴ Round about the throne were four and twenty seats; and upon the seats I saw four and twenty elders sitting clothed in white robes; and they had on their heads crowns of gold. ⁵ And out of the throne proceeded lightnings and thunderings and*

noises; and there were SEVEN LAMPS OF FIRE BURNING BEFORE THE THRONE, WHICH ARE THE SEVEN SPIRITS OF GOD" (Revelation 4.1-5 Aramaic).

Not only are the Seven Spirits of God connected to the seven torches before the throne that can be seen as seven colors of the visible light rainbow; they are also referred to as seven eyes:

"And I beheld, and lo, in the midst of the elders, stood a Lamb as it had been slain, having seven horns and SEVEN EYES, WHICH ARE THE SEVEN SPIRITS OF GOD SENT FORTH INTO ALL THE EARTH" (Revelation 5.6 Aramaic).

"Thus says the Lord of Hosts: If you walk in My ways and keep My commandments, then you shall judge My house and keep My courts, and I will grant you to walk among these that stand by. Hear now, O Joshua, the high priest, you and your fellows who stand before you; [My comment: During the MAJESTIC LIONS - MM Group Ascension on Sept 12, 2016 the group encountered the first High Priest Aaron and we got clothed in high priestly garments. We heard: "priestly skin. You are one with the High Priestly Garment."] *for you are marvelous men: Behold, I will bring forth the rising of the sun upon My servant. For behold, the stone* [Hebrew word for stone is *"even."* It is a conjunction of the words Father *"av"* and Son *"ben"*] *that I have laid before Joshua* [i.e., Yeshua]*; UPON ONE STONE SHALL BE SEVEN FACETS* [i.e., eyes]*; behold, I will open its gates says the LORD of Hosts, and I will remove the iniquity of that land in that day. In that day, says the LORD of Hosts, every man shall invite his neighbor under the vine and under the fig tree"*

(Zechariah 3.7-10 ₐᵣₐₘₐᵢ꜀) *(Zechariah 3.7-10 Aramaic).*

The day when iniquity is completely removed from your land (you) is portrayed on the last great day of the Feast of Tabernacles, which is prophetically portraying you as His Dwelling Place with a river of life flowing from your belly (i.e., innermost being). The last great day of the Feast of Tabernacles is always held on the 22nd of the 7th month. Hummm… speaks about the manifestation of the 22/7 relation of Pi.

When John the Apostle turned to see the voice that spoke to him, he saw seven golden candlesticks: *"12 And I turned to see the voice that spake with me. And being turned I saw seven golden candlesticks; 13 And in the midst of the seven golden candlesticks one like unto the Son of Man"* (Revelation 1.12-13a ₖⱼᵥ). The *Alef/Tav* (i.e., Alpha and Omega) is not seated on a throne when we first see Him in the Book of Revelation, but in the midst of seven golden candlesticks, which we are told are the seven churches (Revelation 1.20). This means that the First and the Last is in the midst of the Body of Christ.

5 -METATRON

METATRON is not an archangel as many have assumed. Metatron is an angel called the Prince of the Presence… Prince of the Dwelling Presence of God… Prince of the Shekinah Glory.

The LORD has told me recently that HE is raising up a Metatron Merkabah Army.

That's why the fifth MEL GEL Class is tapping into Metatron while our sixth class will delve into the Merkabah.

Let's dive right into these deep waters by reading Chapters 3-7 of the Book of Third Enoch [my comments in brackets]:

Chapter 3.

R. Ishmael said:

At that time I asked Metatron, the angel, the prince of the presence, "What is your name?"

He answered, "I have seventy names, corresponding to the seventy languages of the world and all of them are based on the name Metatron, angel of the Presence. However, my King calls me "Youth."

Chapter 4.

R. Ishmael said:

I asked Metatron, "Why does your Creator call you by seventy names? You are more important than all the princes, higher than all the angels, more loved than all the servants. More honored than all the mighty, great, and splendid ones in kingly positions, so why do they call you 'Youth' in the high heavens?"

He answered, "Because I am Enoch, the son of Jared. When the people-group of the Flood sinned and did confused things, they said to Yahweh, 'Leave us, we don't want to know about you.' (Job 21.14), then the Sacred One— may He be blessed! — removed me from them to be a witness against them in the high heavens to all the inhabitants of the earth, so they wouldn't say, 'The Merciful One is cruel.'"

"What sin had all those multitudes committed, they, their wives, their sons, their daughters, their horses, their mules, their cattle, their property, and all the animals wild and domesticated, and the birds of *the world, which the Sacred One – may He be blessed! – destroyed off the face of the earth in the flood waters? What did they do that they would die along with them?*

"And so the Sacred One – may He be blessed! – lifted me up in their lifetime before their eyes to be a witness against them to the future world. And the Sacred One – may He be blessed! – assigned me to be a prince and a ruler among the ministering angels.

At that time three of the ministering angels, Uzza, Azza, and Azazel, came out and brought charges against me in the high heavens. They said in the presence of the Sacred One – may He be blessed! – 'Didn't the First Ones rightly say in Your Presence, 'Do not create humans!' The Sacred One – may He be blessed – answered them, 'I have made you and I will support you. I will carry you and I will rescue you.' (Isaiah 46.4) As soon as they saw me, they said in His Presence, 'Lord of the Universe! Isn't he one from among those who perished in the days of the Flood? What is he doing in Raqia?' Again, the Sacred One – may He be blessed! – answered them, 'Who do you think you are, that you enter and speak in My Presence! I am happier with this one than with all of you, and so he will be a prince and ruler over you in the high heavens!'

So then they all stood up and went out to meet me. They prostrated themselves before me and said, 'You are blessed and your father is blessed because your Creator favors you!'

And because I am small and a youth in comparison with them with regard to days, months and years, this is the reason that they call me 'Youth.'"

Chapter 5.

R. Ishmael said:

Metatron, the Prince of the Presence, said to me:

From the day when the Sacred One— may He be blessed! — expelled the first human from the Garden of Eden and thereafter, Shekinah was residing upon a cherub under the Tree of Life, the ministering angels were gathering and going down from heaven in groups, from the Raqia [high heaven] *in companies, and from the heavens in camps, to do His will throughout the whole world* [This is what Mystic Mentoring Group Ascensions do!!! Groups in companies from the heavens in camps do the Father's perfect will, and Shekinah resides upon us the One New Man in Christ Living Creature... the Cherubim... the Cherubim classification of the Order of Melchizedek. Four people being made in God's image are four living creatures who each have four faces: *"And EVERY ONE HAD FOUR FACES, and every one had four wings" (Ezekiel 1.6 ₖⱼᵥ)*. These four faces for each person in the Living Creature Formation can be classified as the Four Faces of God or as the Four Faces of Melchizedek – lion, ox, eagle man: *"As for the likeness of their faces, they four had the face of a man, and the face of a lion, on the right side: and they four had the face of an ox on the left side; they four also had the face of an eagle" (Ezekiel 1.10 ₖⱼᵥ)*. Please notice that when man (i.e., Israel) sinned, the face of the ox (representative of the Father) was replaced with the cherub: *"And every one had four faces: the first face was the face of the cherub, and the second face was the face of a man, and the third face of a lion, and the fourth face of an eagle" (Ezekiel*

10.14 *KJV*). This is why the priest has to go back up. Melchizedek Priests have to ascend to re-establish the Face of the Ox in their own life. They have to connect to their incredible Heavenly Father to be made whole again. But there is another astounding dimension to the face of the ox being replaced by the cherubim. Ezekiel chapter 10 tells us that the four faces in Ezekiel 1 – lion, ox, eagle and man – are the same faces that are in Ezekiel 10 – lion, cherub, eagle and man: *"And the likeness of their faces was the same faces which I saw by the river Chebar, their appearances and themselves" (Ezekiel 10.22 KJV)*. What this can mean is that the Cherubim, which is a Corporate Order of Melchizedek, is the same as the face of the ox. The ox is the face of the Father, which is why MM Group Ascensions set their focus on the Father (John 5.30; Romans 12.2). A group becomes the Cherubim Classification of the Order of Melchizedek when they focus on the perfect heart of the Father, or in other words, the perfect will of the Father.]

And the first human and the first human's people were sitting outside the gate of the garden to look at the radiant appearance of the Shekinah. For the splendor of the Shekinah went over the world from one end to the other with a radiance 365,000 times that of the sun's orb. No flies and no gnats rested on anyone who made use of the splendor of the Shekinah, and they did not become ill nor did they suffer any pain. No demon got power over them and they were not able to injure them.

When the Sacred One – may He be blessed! – went out and in from the Garden of Eden, from Eden to the Garden, from the Garden to

Raqia and from Raqia to the Garden of Eden, then certainly everyone saw the splendor of His Shekinah, and they were not harmed, right up to the time of the generation of Enosh who was the chief of all idol worshipers of the world. [Notice the connection between the departure of God's Dwelling Presence (Shekinah) and idolatry. See Ezekiel 8.]

And what did the generation of Enosh do? They went from one end of the world to the other, and each one brought silver, gold, precious stones, and pearls in huge heaps like mountains and hills. They made idols out of them throughout the whole world. They erected the idols in every quarter of the world. The size of each idol was 1,000 parasangs. They brought down the sun, the moon, planets and constellations, and placed them before the idols on their right hand and on their left, to attend them just as they attend the Sacred One – may He be blessed! – as it is written (1 Kings 22.19), "All the armies of heaven were standing next to him on his right hand and on his left."

What power did they have that they were able to bring them down? They would not have been able to bring them down but for Uzza, Azza, and Azazel, who taught them sorceries, by which means they brought them down and made use of them.

In that time the ministering angels brought charges against them before the Sacred One – may He be blessed! – and said in His Presence, "Master of the World! What are you going to do with the humans?" As it is written (Psalm 8.4), "What is humankind, that you should notice them, human beings, that you should pay attention to them." Adam is not written here, but Enosh, for Enosh was the chief of the idol worshipers.

Why have you left the Highest of the High heavens which are full of Your splendor and the high exalted Throne in high Araboth, and gone to live with the humans who worship idols and consider idols equal to you! Now You are on earth and so are the idols. What are You going to do with the inhabitants of the earth who worship idols?"

Then the Sacred One – may He be blessed! – took His Shekinah from the earth, away from them. At that moment, the ministering angels arrived, the troops of armies, and the armies of Araboth. A thousand camps and ten thousand hosts arrived. They fetched trumpets and took the horns in their horns in their hands and surrounded the Shekinah with all types of songs. He ascended to the high heavens, as it is written (Psalm 47.5), "Elohim ascended amid a shout, Yahweh amid the sound of a ram's horn."

Chapter 6.

R. Ishmael said:

Metatron, the angel, the Prince of the Presence, said to me:

"When the Sacred One – may He be blessed – wished to lift me up on high, he first sent Anaphiel the Prince. He took me from amongst them right in their sight. He carried me with great splendor on a fiery chariot with fiery horses. He lifted me up to the high heavens together with the Shekinah. As soon as I reached the high heavens, the Sacred Chayyoth [Living Creature/Living Being], *the Ophanin* [wheels], *the Seraphim, the Cherubim, the Wheels of the Merkabah (the Galgallim), and the ministers of the consuming fire, becoming aware of my smell from a distance of 365,000 times many thousands*

of parasangs, said, 'What's that smell of one born of woman! What taste of a white drop of semen is this, that he ascends to the high heavens to minister among those who divide flames of fire!'

The Sacred One — may He be blessed — answered them, 'My servants, My armies, My Cherubim, My Ophanin, My Seraphim! Do not be unhappy about this! Since all the humans have denied me and my great kingdom and have taken up worshipping idols, I have removed My Shekinah from them and have lifted it up on high. But this one whom I have taken from among them is a chosen one among the inhabitants of the world! He is equal to all of them put together with regard to faith, justice and good deeds, and I have taken him as a tribute from My world under all the heavens." [Enoch didn't worship idols. No mixture, including sun god worship, i.e., Christmas. Consider this twisted counterfeit. It's not a coincidence that Metatron has been identified with the Persian sun god Mithra (i.e., celebration of Christmas Day) … mankind's effort to co-opt and corrupt Metatron's functions of Guardian of the World, Mediator for the Earth, Prince of the Word, and witness of all thoughts, words, and actions. There will be more on this soon, because it's crucial to the Shekinah Presence resting on you, which is a key to you taking on your cherubic nature.]

Chapter 7.

R Ishmael said:

Metatron, the angel, the Prince of the Presence, said to me:

When the Sacred One – may He be blessed! – took me away from the generation of the flood, He lifted me on the wings of the wind of Shekinah to the highest heaven and brought me into the great palaces of the high Araboth Raqia, where are the splendid Shekinah, the Merkabah, the angry troops, the vehement armies, the fiery flames, the troops of rage, the armies of vehemence, the fiery Shinanim, the flaming Cherubim, and the burning Ophanin, the flaming servants, the flashing Chashmattim and the lightning Seraphim. He placed me there to attend the splendid Throne day after day.

Descriptors of Metatron in 3 Enoch:

- Metatron is the angel who's called the prince of the presence. The *Jewish Encyclopedia* says that Metatron is also known as:

  o Prince of God's Face (2 Enoch 22)

  o Prince of the Torah [Word of God – Yeshua – Messiah]

  o Prince of Wisdom – "Enoch was translated to heaven to be a witness that God was not cruel. There all the gates of wisdom were opened unto him. As Metatron, he was appointed chief of all the angels, and his carnal body was changed into one of light" *(Hekalot Rabbati).*

  o Prince of Reason

  o Prince of Glory [i.e., Shekinah – Love the Word

until you bind with the Shekinah]

- 3 Enoch 3-4: Metatron has seventy names, corresponding to the seventy languages of the world and all of them are based on the name Metatron, the angel of the presence.

  [My comment – Some say Metatron has 72 names (that we know of). 70 is closely related to 72. "70" is connected to the *Tsadik* – the Righteous Ones. Look up the 70 palm trees in Scripture. "71" is connected to *The Great Tsadik*, which is the Son of God. See Hebrews 7:3. "72" is connected to the complete body, which is Israel and the Bride. We are each one piece of a greater soul – a Bridal Soul. In a sense, we may appear insignificant individually, yet the Body of Christ is not complete without you. You and I have a profound impact on the entirety.]

  [My comment – "72" is connected to the 72 universal laws and the Sapphire Cube. 72 laws are related to the Sabbath (Absolute) Rest. We need to integrate the 72 laws within ourselves. There are 72 dimensions that are not sequential that a person's soul can descend into, go back up; then it all folds into one, which is 144 – the Bridal Soul. A person always starts with the dimension they are operating in. Note that within each dimension are ten spheres.

The Melchizedek Breastplate, which isn't a breastplate at all, becomes the Great Sapphire, the Great City, the City of God, the Great Sapphire City, the Catch – the Messiah.

On the Sapphire Cube are six faces, which are representative of the Great Sapphire City, which represents the multiplicity of one's soul.

There are keys to stepping into the divine space called the City of God – the six-sided Sapphire Cube:

(1) <u>Topmost</u> – Belief in God and love of God, which is the heavenly Zion.

(2) <u>Bottommost</u> – The love and authority of God on earth.

(3) <u>Front Face</u> – The Shema (hear, understand and do), which is connected to the unity of God. This is equivalent to the Face of Man.

(4) <u>Right Side</u> – The love for others, man, dominion, and self. Equivalent to the Face of the Eagle, which is a new perspective from above

(5) <u>Left Side</u> – Awe and thanksgiving. Equivalent to the Face of the Ox.

(6) <u>Back Face</u> – Guards all the gates, great authority and righteousness. It's a shield and

related to abiding in Him. Equivalent to the Face of the Lion.]

- <u>3 Enoch 3</u>: Metatron's King (Creator) calls him "Youth" in the high heavens, because in Metatron Enoch's own words "I am small and a youth" compared to the ministering angels (i.e., the First Ones). [My comment – A son.]

- <u>3 Enoch 4</u>: Metatron is more important than all the princes, higher than all the angels, more loved than all the servants, more honored than all the mighty, great, and splendid ones in kingly positions.

- <u>3 Enoch 4</u>: Metatron is Enoch, the son of Jared, seventh from Adam. The father of Methuselah. Lived 365 years on earth. Pious worshipper of God removed from the dwellers on earth to heaven, receiving the names (offices) of Metatron and *Safra Rabba* – The Great Scribe (*Targum Pseudo-Jonathan*).

- <u>3 Enoch 4</u>: When the generations of The Flood said, "Leave us, we don't want to know about You," the Sacred One removed Enoch from them to be a witness against them in the high heavens to all the inhabitants of earth, so that they wouldn't say, "The Merciful One is cruel." The Sacred One lifted Enoch up in their lifetime before their eyes to be a witness against them to the future world.

[My comment – Enoch is a first fruit of the firstfruits to be removed from the earth before their very eyes.]

- 3 Enoch 4: Melchizedek Enoch was assigned to be a prince and ruler among the ministering angels in the high heavens. The Sacred One was happier with Enoch than with all the ministering angels.

- 3 Enoch 4: The Creator favors Metatron (Enoch).

[My comment – Enoch ended up receiving praise and honor from other angels. His flesh turned into flame and Enoch became the highest angel. Ezekiel 1 reveals a similar description. It is the process we are being taken through where we will be eventually be taken by God sovereignly and transfigured. We prepare for this by taking on our own cherubic nature through the process of descension and ascension (i.e., The *Merkabah* Process). The *Merkabah*'s descension process is especially essential. This is where each of us examine who we truly are in our Kingdom of God within until all layers of our soul integrate with righteousness, holiness and truth. Just so you know, witchcraft eliminates looking at oneself and working to be more like Yeshua.]

- 3 Enoch 6: The Sacred One first sent Anaphiel the Prince to take Enoch right in their sight. Enoch was carried on a fiery chariot with fiery horses to the high heavens together with the Shekinah.

- 3 Enoch 7: When Enoch was taken away by the Sacred One, God lifted Enoch on the wings of the wind of Shekinah to the highest heaven. Enoch was brought into the great palaces of the high heavens – *Raqia* – where the splendid Throne of Shekinah and the Merkabah, et cetera, is. It's the place to attend the splendid Throne (do His will) day after day.

- Therefore, another interpretation for Metatron, the angel, the Prince of the Presence is Metatron, the angel, the prince of the Shekinah Dwelling Presence of God.

NOTE: *Metranoma* is a name given to Shekinah.

If there is one message that I was sent to the world to give, it's that there is a Crux for God's Dwelling Presence that will determine whether you will take on your cherubic nature (first created/primordial state) or not. A "crux" is a puzzling or difficult problem, or an essential point requiring resolution.

What does Scripture say is needed for the Lord's special dwelling presence to stay? His shekinah literally requires holiness. People have tried to make holiness a formula of do's and don'ts, but that will always miss the mark because holiness is a love issue. Doing what Scripture prescribes for holiness taps into the prerequisites for which God's Presence can dwell among us, but we must always take into account that His people's hearts must be totally engaged when we seek to lovingly obey Him.

Believers in the God of Abraham, Isaac and Jacob need to consider that the shekinah glory dwelt in the midst of Israel for generations: *"The people of Israel. Theirs is the adoption of sons; theirs the divine glory..." (Romans 9.4).* First-century believers understood the biblical holiness requirements, which facilitated God's dwelling presence. When the Holy Spirit fell at Pentecost, the church experienced His manifest presence. They additionally sustained a multi-generational revival for more than 300 years, because they understood how to live in God's presence.

For the church to sustain His awe-filled dwelling presence today and for people to fully take on their cherubic nature, we need to accurately grasp His minimum requirements for purity and their relevant application in our lives. Please let us learn from history, so we don't repeat it. God's dwelling presence (i.e., Shekinah Glory) departed from the Christian church when the pagan holidays were assimilated into it. Historical proof is seen in the departure of daily miracles from among them. Scriptural proof is spelled out in Ezekiel chapters 8-11. We are not going into this passage in detail today. We did this in *"The Feast"* Class in November 2015. Please check it out on YouTube => https://www.youtube.com/watch?v=QbEuq3Tz2Q8.

As you personally read Ezekiel 8-11, please note that God's presence slowly and sorrowfully departed, for He longs for His people to repent so His presence may return or remain. *"Son of man, do you see what they are doing … things that will drive Me far from My sanctuary?" (Ezekiel 8.6).* The four idolatrous practices listed in Ezekiel 8.3-5, 9-12, 14, 16 originated in Babylon, and the Bible says that they are detestable to God. Also notice that these all have to do with pure worship. We will only peek at the fourth and most detestable practice in His eyes that drives Him far from His sanctuary: *"So He brought me into the inner court of the LORD's house; and there, at the door of the temple of the LORD, between the porch and the altar, were about twenty-five men with their backs toward the temple of the LORD and their faces toward the east, and they were worshiping the sun toward the east" (Ezekiel 8.16 NKJV).*

The fourth and most detestable practice was performed in the inner court of the house of the Lord between the porch and the altar. The inner court symbolizes those who are intimately acquainted with God. The porch is a place of traversing back and forth. It can be akin to a heaven and earth connection. The altar was a platform of sacrificial worship, where worshipers endeavored to meet with their God. So these twenty-five or so men, who were bowing down to the sun with their backs toward the temple of the Lord, were His close companions. They were people who knew and loved the Lord; yet they still grievously bowed down to and worshiped the sun, whether they acknowledged the fact or not.

The pagans in the fourth century recognized their own solar cults in the church's adoption of the Nativity of the Unconquered Sun (Mithra's Winter Festival). They recognized the church assimilation of their pagan practices in the orienting cathedrals to the east, worshiping on "sun day," and celebrating the birth of the sun god deity at the Winter Solstice. Throughout antiquity, all sun gods across all cultures celebrated their birthday on the ancient winter solstice – December 25th – before the Roman shift in time. *The Catholic Encyclopedia* even documents that the Nativity or Mithra's Winter Festival has a strong claim on our December 25th date. Never mind the fact that Constantine had the Vatican built atop the hill where the Mithra's cult worshiped the sun. History records that it had become common practice in the fifth century for worshipers entering St. Peter's Basilica in Rome to turn at the door, put their backs to the altar, and bow down to worship the rising sun.

Yeshua told me: "Christmas will be the golden calf of America," which means it's idolatry in His eyes. The Lord has given each of us the responsibility to prepare a place for Him: *"When He appears, we shall be like Him; for we shall see Him as He is. Everyone who has this hope in Him purifies himself, just as He is pure" (1 John 3.2-3).* His shekinah glory cannot dwell where there is idolatry; therefore, His dwelling presence cannot, and will not, coexist with this golden calf we call Christmas. Idolatry is the crux that determines whether His shekinah glory will merely visit His people or dwell among them... and it is essential to lay down all idolatry to take on your cherubic nature, like Enoch did. If it's your heart-of-hearts to participate in the fullness of God's glorious Melchizedek and Bridal companies, you will have to pass through this fire.

The four abominations in Ezekiel chapter 8 that drive God's Dwelling Presence far from His sanctuary map to the four faces of God (Melchizedek). To the degree that we compromise with the four abominations is the degree that we don't operate in the fullness of the Cherubim Classification of the Order of Melchizedek. Christmas Day is rooted in the sun god worship of Mithra (Mithraism). It is not a coincidence that the centerpiece of every Mithraeum was a sculptor of Mithras killing a sacred bull. The Worship of Mithra compromises the face of the ox (Father), which the Cherubim (Corporate Order of Melchizedek) is supposed to operate in. The Pattern Son – Yeshua – descended and ascended to take captivity captive. Each Melchizedek Priest has to bring this Christmas Worship issue before the Lord when they descend into the throne within, then once rectified they can ascend to re-establish the Face of the Ox (Father God) to be made whole.

Christmas is the ultimate crux for God's Dwelling Presence that will determine whether you will take on your cherubic nature, or not. And... you get to choose. Please recall that we just read how everyone saw the splendor of His Shekinah until the time of the generation of Enosh when they erected idols in every quarter of the world and brought down THE SUN, the moon, planets and constellations and placed them before their idols.

Christmas has two immediate predecessors:

(1)   CHRISTMAS DAY – Mithra's Winter Festival is also called "The Nativity" or "The Nativity of the Sun" or "The Nativity of the Unconquered Sun"

(2)   CHRISTMAS SEASON – Roman Saturnalia, which was the worship of the pagan god Saturn. The Golden Calf represented the divinity of the ancient Chaldean God Saturn.

The pagan Romans said Saturn was the god of agriculture and time, which brings us back to Metatron.

Metatron whirlwinds together and step in... step into the zero point, which is the midst of the *Merkabah*, where all the waves of energy come in and out... This is the place where we have access to Him... access to the infinite potential that comes from YHVH. Also, remember that Metatron has been identified with the Persian Pagan Sun God Mithra in man's effort to co-opt and control Metatron and his functions as the Guardian of the World, Mediator for the Earth, Prince of the Word (Love of the Word of God [Alef-Tav]) until you bind with *Shekinah*], and witness of all thoughts, words, and actions. In Hebrew Mysticism, some believe Metatron is identical to the Logos, which corresponds to Metatron being the Heavenly One New Man in the Messiah (Christ).

Here's the truth of the matter – Metatron cannot be co-opted. It can be twisted, but not co-opted. Metatron means power or force. Metatron, the Prince of the Presence, is not necessarily a person, but an energetic force. Prophets, priests and kings are people; but Metatron is not a person, but more like a house that houses an energetic force. It's a multiplicity of beings. When we go through the process of ascension and descension, we go into "before the foundations of the world" where everything's already accomplished. We are becoming aware of that eternal reality and bringing it all in to become a kind of new person – united across the grid of the One New Man in Christ.

Metatron is an energetic power or force that's a Being, which is a legion of beings. Metatron is Melchizedek. Metatron is Enoch. Metatron is Elijah. Metatron is Ezekiel. Metatron is David… and so on. Metatron is a multiplicity of beings. It is the literal manifestation of the heavenly One New Man in Christ (in the Messiah).

Metatron is the undifferentiated state of the Messiah – Mature Head with the Transfigured/Transformed Cherubic Body of Christ. We can be and are part of the One New Man in Christ on earth, but Metatron consists of people who have literally become just like Jesus… transfigured/transformed fully mature cells of the fully Mature Body of Christ attached to the Fully Mature Head – Yeshua Messiah.

God abides in you. Now it's your job to abide in Him. Metatron and Melchizedek are various forms so bonded with the spiritual (God) that they begin to be in the spiritual realm fully and are always resonating at His perfect frequency. An oracle abides in God continually and speaks just like God.

Metatron went before Israel in the Wilderness. The Pillar of Cloud and the Pillar of Fire was a whirlwind that formed Solomon's Seal – the Star of David – the Merkabah. The wheels of God's Chariot Throne (Ezekiel) are in charge of the angelic host within and without.

In Chapter 4 of the Third Book of Enoch, Rabbi Ishmael asks: *"Why do they call you 'YOUTH' in the high heavens?"* METATRON answers, *"Because I AM ENOCH, THE SON OF JARED."* Then Chapter 4 goes on to reveal that because, *"I am small and a youth in comparison with the First Ones with regard to days, months and years, this is the reason that they call me YOUTH."* The "Youth" METATRON *was lifted up by the Sacred One before their eyes* [my comment - generation just prior to the Flood] *to be a witness against them to the future world (3 Enoch 4)*. Enoch's function as a "witness" is an essential part of him being a heavenly scribe. He is also called the great scribe, mighty scribe, or angelic golden scribe.

The Order of Melchizedek operates from the governmental seat of rest. On the Youth Metatron is inscribed seven voices: the Seven Spirits of God, which are equivalent to the Shekinah. He is the Prince of the Presence after all. God says: My Name is in His midst. The greatest and most lovely name YHVH is missing the letter SHIN. This SHIN is the Messiah (Mature Body and Mature Head). This is the heavenly man who comes IN the Name of YHVH and is in His midst – Y-H-Shin-V-H. Metatron's body resembles a rainbow – the Shekinah Dwelling Presence of God represented in the Seven Spirit of God – and fire encloses all around.

The Youth Metatron is the manifestation of the Son of God – the Messiah – which bows before His Name and enters beneath the Throne of Glory. The One without a face sustains him. This is the generation that will manifest the full body of the Son of God, which resonates at the frequency of the Torah, which is the Word of God. The Son of God is the living eternal being. Hebrews 7.3 Melchizedek will be made like unto the Son of God.

Metatron appears and only comes by the authority of YHVH. Metatron bears the Tetragrammaton YHVH *(Exodus 23.21) "My Name is IN him,"* yet he may not be worshiped. According to Ariel Kaplan, "Behold God's

Name *El Shaddai* is Metatron." The numerical value of the letters in the word "Metatron" correspond with those of the word "Shaddai," which is 314 that reduces down to 8. The sound of the Living Creature's wings is as the voice of the Almighty (Ezekiel 1.24). *Ezekiel 10.5* says: *"The sound of the Cherubim's wings was heard even to the outer court, as the voice of the Almighty God when He speaks."* Remember on Metatron is inscribed the seven voices of the Seven Spirits of God; therefore, the Metatron Merkabah Army has the voice of the Almighty God and the Seven Spirits of God. This is the voice of *Shaddai* (Almighty God) and *Shekinah* (Dwelling Presence/Glory of God).

Enoch is a first fruit of firstfruits. He is a type and shadow of what is to be made manifest in our day. Soon God is going to take people who walk with Him, the way He took Enoch… but this time, unlike Enoch, His Metatron Merkabah Army will perpetually reside both in heaven and on earth, which is a slight modification to what Enoch experienced: *"Enoch was born on the sixth day of the month of Tsivan, and lived for 365 years. He was taken up to heaven on the first day of the month Tsivan and stayed in heaven 60 days. He wrote about all these signs of creation, which the Lord created, and wrote 366 books. He handed them over to his children and remained on earth for 30 days, after which he was again taken up to heaven on the sixth day of the month Tsivan, on the very day and hour when he was born."* (3 Enoch 68).

The math doesn't add up here. 1 Sivan + 60 days in heaven + 30 days on earth = 6 Sivan?

Like the movie *Interstellar* time is calculated differently in heaven than it is on earth. Expect that the transformed Metatron Merkabah Army will be in heaven a different amount of time than Enoch due to them not exclusively going back into heaven after 30 days on earth; and expect the time spent in the tenth heaven (if Enoch is our example – 2 Enoch 22) to be calculated differently than here on earth... say 20 minutes in heaven is perhaps like 10 years here on earth.

METATRON'S CUBE (c=13) – According to *Jain108 Mathemagics*, the number "13" was made invisible (swept under the carpet). It was deleted from school books. It was given bad press and we were taught to be feared, because its 13 circles (6 around the 1 and another 6 around that) is the fundamental blueprint for all atomic structure. From this matrix (womb of creation) of 13 spheres, all the five Platonic Solids can be created. All the Platonic Solids are the basic geometries of life in all levels of reality. [*¹ From of old God spoke to our fathers by the prophets in every manner and on all ways; and in these latter days he has spoken to us by His Son. ² Whom He has appointed heir of all things, and by whom also He made the worlds; ³ For He is the brightness of His glory and the express image of His being, upholding all things by the power of His word; and when He had through His person cleansed our sins, then He sat down on the right hand of the Majesty on high;* [4] *And He is altogether greater than the angels, just as the name He has inherited is a more excellent name than theirs." (Hebrews 1:1-4* Aramaic*)*]

According to Pistis Sophia (Hurtak), the 13-atom configuration is a cipher for reprogramming and regenesis (i.e., the restoration of all things). Metatron's Cube that has 13 circles that creates five Platonic Solids is also called the Fruit of Life. The Fruit of Life is one of the developmental stages of the Flower of Life, which is the blueprint of creation based on the unchanging radius that walks its circumference to create hexagonal geometry with 72 components in the overall design. The Flower of Life is seen on many ancient temples and architectures, carved or lasered into stone. Other developmental stages of the Flower of Life are the Seed of Life having seven circles, and the Fruit of Life (Metatron's Cube) having 13 circles.

Proverbs 8.27 says: *"When He prepared the heavens, I was there: when He set a compass (circle) upon the face of the deep."* Within Metatron's Cube is the multi-faceted wisdom of God. *The Resonance Project* reveals that the structure of Space-Time is literally a quantized infinite scalar Flower of Life lattice. *"Behold, He stands behind the wall, He looks forth at the windows, showing Himself through the lattice. My Beloved spoke, and said unto me, Rise up, My love, My fair one, and come away" (SS 2.9-10).* Time is a spirally whirlwind and space itself is made of discrete super-tiny packets of energy, which is the smallest little vibration that the electromagnetic spectrum manifests. These tiny packets are what you could think of as pixels that make up the universe. These tiny packets of energy are spherical.

6 – MERKABAH

The word "*Merkabah*" is the Hebrew word for God's Chariot Throne that's featured in Ezekiel 1. The word "*Merkabah*" is not in Scripture, it's simply a description of it.

Question: Who is the Throne of God?

Answer: Man (we are)

The *Merkabah* – God's Chariot Throne – is about the perfection of man, and the Order of Melchizedek is an Order of Perfection.

The *Merkabah* is about changing your Kingdom of God within through the work of Yeshua (Jesus):

"*20 Now when He was asked by the Pharisees when the kingdom of God would come, He answered them and said, 'The Kingdom of God does not come with observation* [inspection, stand by and watch with one's eyes]; *21 nor will they say, 'See here!' or 'See there!' FOR INDEED, THE KINGDOM OF GOD IS WITHIN*

YOU. *22 Then He said to the disciples, 'The days will come when you will desire to see one of the days of the Son of Man, and you will not see it. 23 And they will say to you, 'Look here!' or 'Look there!' Do not go after them or follow them. 24 For as the lightning that flashes out of one part under heaven shines to the other part under heaven, so also the Son of Man will be in His day.* ["For as the lightning comes from the east and flashes to the west, so also will the coming of the Son of Man be" (Matt 24.27 NKJV). Connected to the Four Faces of the Living Creature – Four Faces of God – Four Faces of Melchizedek – four compass points] *25 But first He must suffer many things and be rejected by this generation. 26 And as it was in the days of Noah, so it will be also in the days of the Son of Man:* [This is not about the rapture, which is a false doctrine of escaptology invented by John Darby in 1830. "37 But as the days of Noah were, so also will the coming of the Son of Man be. 38 For as in the days before the flood, they were eating and drinking, marrying and giving in marriage, until the day that Noah entered the Ark, 39 and did not know until the flood came and took them all away, so also the coming of the Son of Man be. 40 Then two men will be in the field: one will be taken and the other left. 41 Two women will be grinding at the mill: one will be taken and the other left. 42 Watch therefore, for you do not know what hour your Lord is coming. 43 But know this, that if the master of the house had known what hour the thief would come, he would have watched and not allowed his house to be broken into. 44 Therefore you also be ready, for the Son of Man is coming at an hour you do not expect" (Matt 24.37-44 NKJV)] *27 They ate, they drank, they married wives, they were given in marriage, until the day that Noah entered the ark, and the flood came and destroyed them all. ²⁸ Likewise as it was also in the days of Lot: They ate, they drank, they bought, they sold, they planted, they built; ²⁹ but on the day that Lot went out of Sodom it rained fire and brimstone from heaven and destroyed them all. ³⁰ Even so will it be in the day when the Son of Man is revealed. ³¹ In that day, he who is on the housetop, and his goods are in the house, let him not come down to take them away. And likewise the one who is in the field, let him not turn back, ³² Remember Lot's wife. ³³ Whoever seeks to save his life will lose it, and whoever loses his life will preserve it. ³⁴ I tell you, in that night there will be two men in one bed: the one will be taken and the other will be left. ³⁵ Two women will be grinding together: the one will be taken and the other left. ³⁶ Two men will be in the field: the one will be taken and the other left. ³⁷ And they answered and said to Him, 'Where, Lord?' So He said to them, Wherever the body is, there the eagles will be gathered together" (Luke 17.27-37 NKJV).*

[What body? Hmm… Allow me to propose the fully mature Metatron Body of the Messiah.]

The *Merkabah* is about changing your Kingdom of God within through the work of Yeshua. How do you practically engage Jesus Christ? Through love and holy desire, we are absorbed into (taken into) the Messiah.

WORD OF CAUTION: Never ever elevate a system above Christ.

The Kingdom of God is withIN you:

- *"Christ IN you, the hope of glory"* (Colossians 1.27).

- *"He has made everything beautiful in its time. Also, He has put eternity IN their hearts, except that no one can find out the work that God does from beginning to end"* (Ecclesiastes 3.11 *NKJV*).

- *" 21 That they all may be one, as You Father are IN Me, and I IN You; that they also may be one IN Us, that the world may believe that You sent Me. 22 And the glory which You gave Me I have given them, that they may be one just as We are one: 23 I IN them and You IN Me; that they may be MADE PERFECT IN ONE, and that the world may know that You have sent Me, and have loved them as You have loved Me. 24 Father, I desire that they also whom You gave Me may be with Me where I am, that they may behold My glory [shekinah] which You have given Me; for You loved Me before the foundation of the world. 25 O righteous Father! The world has not known You, but I have known You; and these have known that You sent Me. 26 And I have declared to them Your name, and will declare it, that the love with which You loved Me may be IN them, and I IN them"* (John 17.21-26 *NKJV*).

Everything is created IN. The heavenly position of being "IN CHRIST" is the complete replacement of the man of sin in its fullness. Completely being IN CHRIST (on earth as it is in heaven) happens when your heavenly position purchased on the cross by the shed blood of Jesus [100 percent "in Christ"] becomes your earthly condition [percentage you manifest your "in Christ" heavenly position on earth].

The Kingdom of God is within you. It is "IN" you. Picture if you will the Lord enthroned in a flame above your heart, like there was a blue flame above the Ark of God's Presence in the Holy of Holies. The four chambers of your heart are like the four sides of the Ark of the Covenant. Think of the four chambers also being like Y-H-V-H. The Messiah (Shin) is IN the center of His Name: Y-H-Shin-V-H. The pure and spotless one IN THE NAME is the Bridal Blueprint for the ultimate Dwelling Place of God – The New Jerusalem.

Always remember we seek God inwardly, because the Kingdom of God is already within ("IN") us once we accept Jesus Christ as our Lord and Savior. We focus on the "Shin" (Almighty God – Messiah Yeshua) within with a pure desire based in love, then we are able to move both multi-dimensionally and non-locally. We are able to be anywhere in time and space. We are able to go anywhere, because eternity is IN our hearts (this universe and all universes are within you). Jesus Christ the Son of God activates the *Merkabah*. The *Merkabah* changes you through the work of Yeshua. We want to go into the Kingdom Realm within, not simply go into the spirit.

Question: What is the second letter of the Hebrew Alef-Bet?

Answer: Bet.

Did you know that the letter BET can mean "IN," like "IN THE BEGINNING"? We need to tap into infinity... the "in the beginning" of all creation. Imagination is a handshake between our current capacity and the limitless boundaries of God... the Kingdom of God. You know Albert Einstein said, "Imagination will get you everywhere." Although imagination is used in all forms of ascension, we don't ascend by our imaginations... but by the Holy Spirit.

Since the Cross, God's people rightly ascend and descend through the Cross and the Blood by the Holy Spirit, which takes you into the Door - Jesus Christ, and then the Doorkeeper opens the Door. *" ¹ Most assuredly, I say to you, he who does not enter the sheepfold by the door, but climbs up* [ascension] *some other way, the same is a thief and a robber. ² But he who enters by the door is the shepherd of the sheep. ³ To him the doorkeeper opens, and the sheep hear his voice; and he calls his own sheep by name and leads them out. ⁴ And when he brings out his own sheep, he goes before them; and the sheep follow him, for they know his voice. ⁵ Yet they will by no means follow a stranger, but will flee from him, for they do not know the voice of strangers. ... ⁷ Then Jesus said to them again, 'Most assuredly, I say to you, I am the door of the sheep. ⁸ All who ever came before Me are thieves and robbers, but the sheep did not hear them. ⁹ I AM THE DOOR. IF ANYONE ENTERS BY ME, HE WILL BE SAVED, AND WILL GO IN AND OUT AND FIND PASTURE" (John 10.1-9 NKJV).*

This passage of Scripture happened during Hanukkah – the Feast of Dedication... the Dedication of the Altar... the Dedication of our hearts. When you read John 8.12

through John 10.42, understand that you are reading about the Yeshua's works that happened during Hanukkah. There are thirteen "I AM" statements proclaimed by Yeshua Himself during the Feast of Dedication. Remember the thirteen spheres in Metatron's Cube? Hint. Hint. Within the thirteen "I AM" statements Yeshua proclaimed during Hanukkah are three repeated statements, which includes Jesus putting greater emphasis on "I AM THE DOOR."

[1] <u>I AM THE LIGHT OF THE WORLD</u>:

The first Hanukkah I AM statement is *"I AM THE LIGHT OF THE WORLD. He who follows Me shall not walk in darkness, but have the light of life"* (John 8.12 NKJV). This goes right along with the tenth Hanukkah I AM statement of Yeshua: *"The thief comes not, but to steal, and to kill, and to destroy: I AM come that they might have life, and that they might have it more abundantly"* (John 10.10 KJV). The light of life is connected to abundant life here.

The sixth and seventh Hanukkah I AM Statement are in the same verse: *"As long as I AM in the world, I AM THE LIGHT OF THE WORLD"* (John 9.5 NKJV).

Yeshua Himself fulfilled Hanukkah by decreeing twice during the Feast of Dedication: I AM THE LIGHT OF THE WORLD. Hanukkah is also known as the Feast of Lights and the Feast of Miracles.

[2] I AM THE DOOR:

The eighth Hanukkah I AM statement of Yeshua is: *"Most assuredly, I say to you, I AM THE DOOR of the sheep"* (John 10.7 NKJV), and

The ninth Hanukkah I AM statement is *"I AM THE DOOR. If anyone enter by Me, he will be saved, and will go in and out and find pasture"* (John 10.9 NKJV).

[3] I AM THE GOOD SHEPHERD:

The eleventh Hanukkah I AM statement of Yeshua reveals *"I AM THE GOOD SHEPHERD. The good shepherd gives His life for the sheep"* (John 10.11 NKJV).

The twelfth Hanukkah I AM statement of Yeshua is: *"I AM THE GOOD SHEPHERD; and I know My sheep, and am known by My own"* (John 10.14 NKJV).

"For you had gone astray like sheep, but you have now returned to the Shepherd and the Guardian of your souls" (1 Peter 2.25 Aramaic).

Yeshua proclaims in the thirteenth "I AM" that *"I AM the Son of God"* (John 10.36). Hebrews 7.3 tells us that those made after the Order of Melchizedek are made like unto the Son of God. The Youth Metatron is the actual manifestation of the Son of God in its fullness.

Thirteen "I AM"'s of Yeshua. Recall the 13 circles of Metatron (6 around 1 and another 6 around that), which is a picture of Metatron's Cube. It is a picture of the fundamental blueprint for all atomic structure. Also, recall that Metatron, the Prince of the Presence (Shekinah), is the undifferentiated state of the Messiah, which is the fullness of the heavenly manifestation of the One New Man in Christ (i.e., the Messiah).

Yeshua, who is the Messiah, is seated in heavenly places (Ephesians 2.6). He is the Head of the Body of Christ (Ephesians 4.15).

We know that the Body of Christ is currently in flux. What I mean by that is we currently see various stages of development in the Body of Christ here on earth. Romans 8.19 reveals that all of creation is groaning for the manifestation of the sons of the Living God. They are groaning for those made after the Order of Melchizedek made like unto the Son of God.

The "Youth" Metatron consists of the sons of man who have literally become the sons of God. Understand that Metatron only consists of the Fully Mature Body of Christ connected to the Fully Mature Head of Christ – Yeshua. We can be, and are, part of the One New Man in Christ on earth when we accept the gift of salvation, but Metatron solely consists of people who have literally become just like Jesus in heavenly places. This is one of the reasons that Metatron is called the angel (not an archangel), the Prince of the Presence.

God is raising up a Metatron Merkabah Army. As

Metatron, Enoch is the visible firstfruits forerunner for the heavenly One New Man in Christ. There are more firstfruits to follow. Our next MEL GEL Class subject is about the mystery of the 144,000 Firstfruits.

In the *Sefer Hekalot*, Rabbi Ishmael meets Enoch who had been raised to the dignity of Metatron. *The Jewish Encyclopedia* reveals how Enoch tells R. Ishmael the story of his elevation as follows: in consequence of earth's corruption by the evil spirits Shamhazai and Azazel, Enoch was translated to heaven to be a witness that God was not cruel. There all the gates of wisdom were opened unto him as METATRON, he was appointed chief of all angels, and his carnal body was changed into one of light.

Remember Metatron means power or force. Let's break down the Hebrew word *Merkabah*. *"Mer"* means light. *"Ka"* means Spirit. *"Ba"* means body. Therefore, *Merkabah* refers to a "Light Spirit Body," and Metatron Merkabah is connected to the Power or Force of the Light Spirit Body.

The key to the complete transformation of our bodies into light is hidden within the Biblical Feast of Hanukkah. It's a picture that only the pure in heart can access being transfigured into Sons of Light. The secret is hidden within the Thirteen "I AM" statements Yeshua said during the Feast of Dedication as well as the Ten Copper Chariot Lavers in Solomon's Temple, which is a picture of the Kingdom of God.

The study of the *Merkabah* is considered to be a theosophy. What is theosophy? My *10th Edition Webster's Collegiate*

Dictionary says a theosophy is a teaching about God and the world based on mystical insight.

It's not a coincidence that the sons of the Living God are redeeming Mysticism and the Mystics. The word "mystic" comes from the Latin "mysticus," which means "of mysteries." A mystery is a religious truth that one can know only by revelation and cannot be fully understood. A mystic relates to the mysterious, has a feeling of awe or wonder, and is a follower of the mystical way of life. A mystical way of life is having a spiritual meaning of reality. It involves having direct communion with God or the ultimate reality. Mysticism is the belief that direct knowledge of God, spiritual truth, or ultimate reality can be attained through experience. According to Dr. Elizabeth Petroff, mysticism has been called "the science of the love of God," and "the life which aims at union with God."

The antidote to the *"Mystery of Iniquity" (1 Thess 2.7)*, *"Mystery Babylon" (Rev 17.5)*, and the *"mystery of the woman and the beast" (Rev 17.7)* are literally found in the mysteries of God the Father and of Christ, so let's redeem the Mystic. The Order of Melchizedek restores all things that can be redeemed. Having direct communion with God and His ultimate reality through experience is not only redeemable, it's divine and sublime. Next time you hear the word "mystic" think of knowing the love of God, and displaying this unlimited, exquisite mystery for all to see.

The *Merkabah* Mysteries are all about *Mer* – Light, *Ka* – Spirit, *Ba* – body… Light Spirit Body. The *Merkabah* is the star tetrahedron Light Force, which connects to the light in our DNA. Did you know that our DNA communicates with, and is created from, light itself? Scientists are saying that light appears to be a fundamental part of our being. It's hard-coded into our very bodies to function directly with and through light. We also affect light with our intentions. Remember this, because it is key to the mysteries of the *Merkabah* where a person takes on their cherubic nature.

The only cherubim not in the sanctuary of Solomon's Temple (the House of God itself) are the cherubim engraved on the Ten Copper Chariot Lavers, which are connected to the 10 strands of DNA that were deactivated after The Fall. Just as the Ten Copper Chariot Lavers were dismissed and treated like junk, so has our Ten Shadow (Junk) DNA Strands. This "junk DNA" is actually one of our greatest hidden treasures. God's Chariot Throne – the *Merkabah* – is "the chariot" in which the Ten Copper CHARIOT Lavers operate. The *Merkabah* process is literally the missing link in the Bridal Restoration of our 10-Shadow Strands of DNA.

When we walk in the fullness of the measure of the stature of Christ – Metatron – all 12-Strands of our DNA will be turned on (activated), just like Yeshua when He walked the earth. Can you see the Metatron Merkabah picture starting to form? We have God's Chariot Throne – the Merkabah – with its charioteer – the One New Man in Christ (at various levels) with the ultimate charioteer being Metatron, the multiplicity of beings of the Fully Mature Body of the Messiah connected to the Fully Mature Head of Christ.

Each one of His kings and priests of the Order of Melchizedek are leading their own inner fire bride forth. There are three components that are always present in the perfection of the Order of Melchizedek. They are the three transformative agents that accomplish the Bridal Restoration of our DNA (activating all 12 Strands of our DNA):

[1] Daily Communion,

[2] Daily Crucifixion, and

[3] Daily Bread (the Word of God).

Notice that all three of these components are necessary to truly examine our current earthly condition. The Ten Copper Chariot Lavers in Solomon's Temple are connected to the descension component of the *Merkabah*. Notice that the Ten Copper Chariot Lavers were used to wash the blood from the body of the burnt offerings. The priests could not wash them until the burnt offerings were properly prepared.

Burnt Offerings:

- Voluntary Offering given exclusively to the Lord.

- Also called the Elevation Offering, because it raises one's spiritual level (ascension).

- Considered to be superior to other offerings, because it's a free-will offering brought in its entirety by fire.

- Called an *olah* in Hebrew, which means "to go up."

- *Olah*'s Ancient Hebrew Word Picture tells us that an *olah* is that which the Shepherd brings forth.

- The Great Shepherd of our soul will choose what will best crucify our sin nature.

Conveniently, daily crucifixion is included in daily communion, because genuinely partaking of common union requires us to examine ourselves – our hearts, our attitudes, our deeds and our behaviors. Once the burnt offerings (Great Shepherd chooses what's best for you) get slaughtered (daily crucifixion), the blood gets washed by the water of the word, and the washing of regeneration of the Spirit in these Ten Copper Chariot Lavers (Ephesians 5.26; Titus 3.5).

To return to our primordial Living Being of Light State (i.e., cherubic nature), we have to be transformed through the Blood of Yeshua, and His Body. Daily Communion is all about the body and blood – the Messiah's Body and the Messiah's Blood: *"Then Jesus said to them, 'Most assuredly, I say to you, unless you eat the flesh of the Son of Man and drink His blood, you have no life in you. Whoever eats My flesh and drinks My blood has eternal life, and I will raise him up at the last day. For My flesh is food indeed, and My blood is drink indeed. He who eats My flesh and drinks My blood abides IN Me, and I IN him"* (John 6.53-56 NKJV).

We can only be joined to Christ (the Messiah – insert Metatron here) if we carry His likeness and His 12-Light Strands of DNA. Just want to note here: Ian Clayton teaches that through communion, our bones start producing the correct record in our blood first; then as we make the right choices (reflection, introspection of yourself within the *Merkabah*) our body gets conformed into His image that has been born in our blood first. Basically, it's a Communion - Crucifixion- Word of God process. [Check out *Sapphire Throne Ministries's BLAZING NEW WINE OF HANUKKAH* and *HITTING THE BULL'S EYE OF RIGHTEOUSNESS* books.]

Don't forget that we have a picture of when Enoch's carnal body (mortality) was changed into one of light (took on immortality). This is a *theosis*. A *theosis* is a transformative process whose goal is likeness to, or union with, God. *Theosis* is the understanding that human beings can have real union with God, and so become like God to such a degree that we participate in the divine nature in which we were originally created (Gen 1.26-27). In the fullness of our original divine image, we are a perfect reflection of our God, and partakers of the divine nature (2 Peter 1.4). This is the *Romans 8.23 "redemption of the body."*

The Jewish Encyclopedia says: "In the future [which is now] Ezekiel will come again and unlock for Israel [Is-real] the chambers of the Merkabah" (Cant. R. i. 4).

Let's back up just a bit to lay some fundamental Merkabah ground work. The word Merkabah is the Hebrew word for God's Chariot Throne featured in Ezekiel 1.

Chapter one of the Book of Ezekiel is referred to by the Hebrew Sages as *Maaseh Merkavah* – "The Account of the Chariot." It is also the pattern for Ascension. Let's skip the first three verses, which give the time and place of the vision, to jump right into the *Maaseh Merkavah* vision itself. Notice as we read Ezekiel chapter one that there are three parts to the *Merkabah* – God's Chariot Throne:

[1] the part beneath the firmament – The Four Living Creatures

[2] firmament itself

[3] the part above the firmament – Sapphire Throne.

*****

Ezekiel 1:4-28 Aramaic

⁴And I looked, and behold, a whirlwind was coming out of the north, a great cloud, and a flaming fire and a brightness was round about it, and out of the midst of it there came as it were a figure out of the midst of the fire. ⁵Also out of the midst of it came the likeness of four living creatures. And this was their appearance: they had the likeness of a man. ⁶And every one had four faces, and every one had four wings. ⁷And their legs were straight; and the soles of their feet were like the soles of a calf's feet; and they sparkled like the color of burnished brass. ⁸And they had human hands under their wings on their four sides; and their faces and their wings were on their four sides. ⁹Their wings were joined one to another; and when they went, they were straight forward; they turned not when they went. ¹⁰And as for the likeness of their faces, each of the four had the face of a man and the face of a lion on the right side; and each of the four had the face of the ox and the face of an eagle on the left side. [11] And their faces and their wings were stretched upward; two wings of each creature were joined one to another, and two covered their bodies. [12] And they went every one straight forward; wherever the spirit was to go, they went; and they turned not when they went. [13] As for the likeness of the living creatures, their appearance was like burning coals of fire, like the appearance of a lamp going to and fro among the living creatures; and the fire was bright, and out of the fire went forth lightning. [14] And the living creatures ran, but returned not, and their appearance was like a flash of lightning. [15] Now as I beheld the living creatures, behold wheels were upon the earth by the side of each of the four living creatures. [16] The appearance of the wheels and their work was like the color of a beryl; and they four had the one likeness; and their appearance and their work was as it were a wheel within a wheel. [17] When they went, they went upon four sides; and they turned not when they went; and wherever the first one turned to go, the other went after it, and turned not. [18] As for their rims, they were high and they could see; for the rims were full of eyes round about them four. [19] And when the living creatures went, the wheels went with them; and when the living creatures were lifted up from the ground, the wheels were lifted up with them. [20] Wheresoever the spirit was to go, they went, and the wheels were lifted up with them; for there was a living spirit in the wheels. [21] When the living creatures went, the wheels went; and when the creatures stood, they stood also; and when they were lifted up from the earth, the wheels were lifted up with them; for there was a living spirit in the wheels. [22] And over the heads of the living creatures there was the likeness of a firmament, resembling pure crystal, stretched out over their heads above. [23] And under the firmament were their wings *straight, the one toward the other; over and under; two of them covered their faces and two covered their bodies.* ²⁴*And when they went, I heard the noise of their wings like the nose of great waters, like the voice of God, like the sound of speech in a host; and when they stopped, they let down their wings.* ²⁵*And there was a voice from the firmament that was over their heads; and when they stopped they let down their wings.* ²⁶*And above the firmament that was over their heads was the likeness of a sapphire stone, as the likeness of the throne; and upon the likeness of the throne was the likeness as the appearance of a man above it.* ²⁷*And I saw as it were the appearance of God, and the appearance of fire within it round about from his loins and upward; and from his loins and downward, I saw as it were the appearance of fire shining round about.* ²⁸*As the appearance of the rainbow when it is in the clouds in the day of rain, so was the appearance of the brightness round about him. Such was the vision of the likeness of the glory of the LORD. And when I saw it, I fell upon my face and I heard the voice of one who spoke.*

*****

Ezekiel 1:4-28 KJV (The King James Version is the most accurate translation from the confusing Hebrew)

⁴*And I looked, and behold, a whirlwind came out of the north, a great cloud, and a fire infolding itself, and a brightness was about it, and out of the midst thereof as the color of amber, out of the midst of the fire.* ⁵*Also out of the midst thereof came the likeness of four living creatures. And this was their appearance; they had the likeness of a*

man. ^{6}And every one had four faces, and every one had four wings. ^{7}And their feet were straight feet; and the sole of the feet was like the sole of a calf's foot: and they sparkled like the color of burnished brass. ^{8}And they had the hands of a man under their wings on their four sides; and they four had their faces and their wings. ^{9}Their wings were joined one to another; they turned not when they went; they went every one straight forward. ^{10}As for the likeness of their faces, they four had the face of a man, and the face of the lion, on the right side: and they four had the face of an ox on the left side; they four also had the face of an eagle. ^{11}Thus were their faces: and their wings were stretched upward; two wings of every one were joined one to another, and two covered their bodies. ^{12}And they went every one straight forward: whither the spirit was to go, they went; and they turned not when they went. ^{13}As for the likeness of the living creatures, their appearance was like burning coals of fire, and like the appearance of lamps: it went up and down among the living creatures; and the fire was bright, and out of the fire went forth lightning. ^{14}And the living creatures ran and returned as the appearance of a flash of lightning. ^{15}Now as I beheld the living creatures, behold one wheel upon the earth by the living creatures, with his four faces. ^{16}The appearance of the wheels and their work was like unto the color of a beryl: and they four had one likeness: and their appearance and their work was as it were a wheel in the middle of a wheel. ^{17}When they went, they went upon their four sides: and they turned not when they went. ^{18}As for their rings, they were so high that they were dreadful; and their rings were full of eyes round about them four. ^{19}And when the living creatures went, the wheels went by them: and when the living creatures were lifted up from the earth, the wheels were lifted up. ^{20}Whithersoever the spirit was to go, they went, thither was their spirit to go: and the wheels were lifted up over against them: for the spirit of the living creature was in the wheels. ²¹ When those went, these went; and when those stood, these stood; and when those were lifted up from the earth, the wheels were lifted up over against them: for the spirit of the living creature was in the wheels. ²²And the likeness of the firmament upon the heads of the Living Creature was as the color of the terrible crystal, stretched forth over their heads above. ²³And under the firmament were their wings straight, the one toward the other: every one had two, which covered on this side, and every one had two, which covered on that side, their bodies. ²⁴And when they went, I heard the noise of their wings, like the noise of great waters, as the voice of the Almighty, the voice of speech, as the noise of a host: when they stood, they let down their wings. ²⁵And there was a voice from the firmament that was over their heads, when they stood, and had let down their wings. ²⁶And above the firmament that was over their heads was the likeness of a throne, as the appearance of a sapphire stone: and upon the likeness of the throne was the likeness as the appearance of a man above upon it. ²⁷And I saw as the color of amber, as the appearance of fire round about within it, from the appearance of his loins even upward, and from the appearance of his lions even downward, I saw as it were the appearance of fire and it had brightness round about. ²⁸As the appearance of the bow that is in the cloud in the day of rain, so was the appearance of the brightness round about. This was the appearance of the likeness of the glory of the LORD. And when I saw it, I fell upon my face, and I heard a Voice of One that spake.

*****

Ezekiel 1:4-28, The Artscroll English Tanach, Stone Edition

"*4 I saw, and behold! there was a stormy wind coming from the north, a great cloud with flashing fire and a brilliance surrounding it; and from its midst, like the color of the Chashmal* [a type of angel that at times stands silent (Hebrew: "chash") and at times speaks (Hebrew: "memaleil") God's praises (Chagigah 13a)] *from the midst of the fire; 5and in its midst there was a likeness of four Chayos* [Lit., living beings (singular, Chayah)]. *This was their appearance: They had the likeness of a man; 6 each one had four faces, and each one of them had four wings; 7 their legs were a straight leg, and the sole of their feet was like the sole of a rounded foot, and they glittered with the color of burnished copper; 8 there were human hands under their wings on their four sides. Their faces and their wings [were alike] on the four of them; 9 their wings were joined to one another. They did not turn as they went; each in the direction of its faces would they go. 10As for the likeness of their faces: There was a human face; and a lion's face to the right for the four of them; and an ox's face to the left for the four of them, and an eagle's face for the four of them. 11As for their faces: Their wings extended upward [over them]; for each [face] two [wings] were joined to each other; and two [wings] were covering their bodies. 12 Each in the direction of its faces would they go; toward wherever there was the spirit to go, they would go; they did not turn as they went. 13As for the likeness of the Chayos: Their appearance was like fiery coals, burning like the appearance of torches; its spread about among the Chayos; there was a brilliance to the fire, and from the fire went forth lightning. 14 The Chayos ran to and fro like the appearance of a flash. 15 I saw the Chayos — and behold! one Ofan* [lit. wheel, a type of celestial being] *was on the surface near [each of] the Chayos by its four faces. 16 The appearance*

127

of the Ofanim and their nature were like the color of tarshish [beryl],
*with the same likeness for the four of them; and their appearance and
their works were as if there would be a wheel within a wheel.* ¹⁷ *When
they went, they would go toward their four sides; they did not turn as
they went.* ¹⁸ *They had backs, and they were tall, and they were
fearsome. Their backs were full of eyes surrounding the four of them.*
¹⁹ *When the Chayos would go, the Ofanim would go next to them,
and when the Chayos were lifted from upon the surface, the Ofanim
were lifted.* ²⁰ *Toward wherever there was the spirit to go, they would
go, [for] there was the spirit to go; the Ofanim were lifted facing them,
for the spirit in the Chayah was [also] in the Ofanim.* ²¹ *When [the
Chayos] would go, [the Ofanim] would go, and when they halted, they
halted; and when they were lifted from upon the surface, the Ofanim
were lifted facing them, for the spirit in the Chayah was [also] in the
Ofanim.* ²² *There was a likeness of an expanse above the heads of the
Chayah, like the color of the awesome ice, spread out over their heads
from above.* ²³ *And beneath the expanse, their wings were even one
with the other; for each [of them] two [wings] covered them, and for
each [of them] two covered them, their bodies.* ²⁴ *I heard the sound of
their wings, like the sound of great waters, like the sound of
SHADDAI* [The Almighty], *as they moved, the sound of a
commotion, like the sound of a camp; when they would halt, they
would release their wings.* ²⁵ *There was a voice from above the expanse
that was over their heads; when they would halt, they would release
their wings.* ²⁶*Above the expanse that was over their heads was the
appearance of sapphire stone in the likeness of a throne, and upon the
likeness of the throne there was a likeness like the appearance of a
man upon it, from above.* ²⁷*And I saw the color of Chashmal, like
the appearance of fire inside it all around, from the appearance of his*

loins and upward; and from the appearance of his loins and downward I saw something like the appearance of fire, and a brilliance surrounding it. ²⁸ Like the appearance of a bow that would be in the clouds on a rainy day, so was the appearance of the brilliance all around. That was the appearance of the likeness of the glory of HASHEM! When I saw, I fell upon my face, and I heard a voice speaking."

Let's look at the Four Faces of the Living Creature, the Four Faces of Melchizedek, or the Four Faces of God.

The Jewish Encyclopedia says: "Concerning the lion, the ox, the eagle and the man as the four faces of the Hayyot [Living Beings] … these four, which carry God's Throne-Chariot." The *Merkabah* (Ezekiel's Chariot Throne) operates on at least three different levels, which can be activated all at the same time.

[1] <u>FOUR FACES OF THE LIVING CREATURE</u>: When a person is born from above, they can see the Kingdom of God (John 3.3). This is when the foundational Kingdom-of-God-Within dynamics are deposited within each person. These Kingdom of God dynamics exist within them here on earth, whether they know it or not. At this first stage of Kingdom of God Within Development, we come to know and realize the four faces within ourselves (within each believer):

1. Man – Body

2. Ox (Cherub) – Soul

3. Eagle – Spirit

4. Lion – Holy Spirit awaken your spirit to the fourth being within you (*shin*). Messiah Yeshua abides in those who accept Him as Lord and Savior. We strive to abide in Christ. By the Holy Spirit, we ascend into Christ.

[2] <u>FOUR FACES OF GOD</u>: When a person is born by water and spirit, they enter the Kingdom of God (John 3.5). This means that a person begins to operate in Kingdom of God dynamics that they have already cultivated as well as having unlimited growth potential. At this second stage of Kingdom-of-God-Within Development, each individual person connects more intimately with the Four Faces of God:

1. Man – One Person (You)

2. Ox (Cherub) – The Father

3. Eagle – Holy Spirit

4. Lion – Jesus (Yeshua)

[3] <u>FOUR FACES OF MELCHIZEDEK</u>: At the third stage of Kingdom-of God-Within Development, a group of four or more people who personally connects to the Four Faces of God unite in order to inherit the Kingdom of God (1 Cor 6.9-10; Gal 5.19-21). Therefore, at this corporate stage, four (or more) people connect in a fourfold way to the Four Faces of Melchizedek:

1. Man – First person united with the Father, the Son and the Holy Spirit

2. Ox (Cherub) – Second person united with the Father, the Son and the Holy Spirit

3. Eagle – Third person united with the Father, the Son and the Holy Spirit

4. Lion – Fourth person united with the Father, the Son and the Holy Spirit

Even though the *Merkabah* is quite ancient, my initial exposure came from God Himself. It happened while I was taking communion one morning with the Father, the Son and the Holy Spirit.

For years before this, I had taken communion daily with Yeshua, as He had divinely initiated around the year 2000. It was a corporate communion time, but the Lord had instructed everyone to look exclusively at Yeshua individually while corporately taking communion. I was bowled over with Yeshua whispering over the bread "with this bread, I thee wed" and over the cup "with this wine, I thee wed." I was in awe, as I repeated after Him. This was a new and life-giving way of taking communion, which grew from the taking of communion to taking on common union (i.e., communion).

Ten years later, the night before my taking on common union shifted into "with this bread and wine, *WE* thee wed," I had cried out from my innermost being that I wanted the seven-fold nature of Christ, which are the Seven Spirits of God that possessed Jesus's soul while He walked on earth, to possess me. I wanted Christ's Being lived out through me by means of the Seven Spirits of God. The next morning, I received a vision of Yeshua walking among the seven torches (Seven Spirits of God) and I heard the Father say: "Today, we come together for holy matrimony." Even though I was a bit perplexed, I immediately quieted myself and listened with great expectation and awe. I saw the four of us – the Father, the Son, the Holy Spirit and myself – sitting around a square table. The Father was directly opposite of me, Yeshua was to my right, and the Holy Spirit to my left. We sat there for a while in conversation; then without any verbal instruction, all of us spontaneously recited in complete unison: "With this bread, we thee wed." We repeated this oneness feat with the wine. After this glorious divine encounter, the Spirit directed me to Ezekiel chapter 1, which I studied with new eyes to see.

It's not a coincidence that I was directed to Ezekiel chapter

1, which reveals the *Merkabah* (God's Chariot Throne), with this new-found way of taking on fourfold divine common union. True communion requires you to examine yourself, so you can move into deeper dimensions within yourself – your Kingdom of God within (Luke 17.21). Interesting enough, so does the *Merkabah* require that a person go deeper and deeper into the Kingdom of God within. When we focus inward and descend into the Holy of Holies there, we are centering in on the Kingdom of God within. This is the pattern for ascension that Yeshua gave us: *"Now that he ascended, what is it but that he also descended first into the lower parts of the earth?" (Ephesians 4.9 KJV).*

The *Merkabah* shows when a person ascends, they first descend to a platform within the heart of their own earth, which then becomes a springboard to ascend. The proper application of the *Merkabah* Process causes you to descend into dimensions that are deeper and deeper within (internally), and to ascend into dimensions higher and higher without (externally). True transformation is always applied to ourselves first before we can affect lasting change externally. Everything you learn ascending and descending contributes to your growth. My advice is to allow God to take you where He wants to take you. He knows the way that we take and how to bring us forth as gold (Job 23.10). Let Him lead you to new dimensions and new realms.

When we descend into Christ (into the Holy of Holies), we become the *Merkabah*. Christ is the *Merkabah*, and in Him

133

we are the *Merkabah*. We are "in Christ" and He is in us. His death is the descension, and His resurrection the ascension.

Notice that descension is pictured as a downward pointing tetrahedron (three-dimensional triangle) rotating counter-clockwise. It's undoing things that need to be rectified in order to be made into the exact same image as Jesus. The ascension is pictured as an upward pointing tetrahedron that's rotating clockwise. It's arising. Notice also the man spinning in the center of the Merkabah (dimensional Star of David).

To fully manifest the glory of God's Chariot Throne – His *Merkabah* – we must continually live in a descended state on this earth as a continual burnt offering as well as continually living in heavenly places in an ascended state. (For more information about becoming a "continual burnt offering," please see *Sapphire Throne Ministries' HITTING THE BULL'S EYE OF RIGHTEOUSNESS* book.) Paul speaks of continually living in a descended state: *"I have been crucified with Christ [in Him I have shared His crucifixion]; it is no longer I who live, but Christ (the Messiah) lives in me; and the life I now live in the body I live by faith in (by adherence to and reliance on and complete trust in) the Son of God, Who loved me and gave Himself up for me"* (Galatians 2.20 *Amplified*).

Descenders who go into the Kingdom of God within are able to go anywhere in time and space, because eternity has been set in our hearts. When you step into Christ, you become non-local because everything is in you.

When you are in proper Divine Right Alignment and your passion is set on constant loving communion with the Most High God, you have a perfect set-up to ride the *Merkabah*. Proper Divine Right Alignment is when your body is submitted to your soul, your soul is submitted to your spirit, and your spirit is submitted to the Holy Spirit. Basically, it's your soul in the spirit riding the *Merkabah*. Since December 2015, many people in the MM Group Ascensions are corporately riding the *Merkabah* where we are ascending with both our souls and our spirits together. We can "feel" when this happens. It feels very floaty or atmospheric in the Spirit. We are pressing in to ascend as a group with our spirits, our souls and our bodies.

Entering the *Merkabah* is simply engaging in an intimate relationship with the lover of your soul. Even though imagination is used in all forms of ascension, it's not your imagination that allows you to ascend. You can ascend rightly only through your right relationship with Christ. Even though we are seated in heavenly places in Christ, His sons also ascend into heaven by the power of the Holy Spirit to discover the reality of who we are and who God is.

The *Merkabah* causes you to descend into a dimension within yourself [firmament – veils or dimensions within you], the dimension in which you currently exist. Through the work of Jesus and the cross, we change that dimension within to be just like Him. You have to change yourself in the dimension that you currently exist to be able to go into another dimension. When we truly discover who we are, we actually discover who God is. Can you see why taking communion is such an important component to the whole process? The *Merkabah* is all about changing you through the work of Yeshua (Jesus).

The *Merkabah* causes you to first descend – "scuba dive" in the Spirit – to the level you currently exist; then you look for Yeshua (or YHVH) on that level, ask Him to show you your reflection in that place, and choose to repent for anything not resonating at the frequency of the Word in order to change that dimension into gold.

The *Merkabah* can operate on an individual level or on a corporate level. Once you unite in oneness with the Father, Son and Holy Spirit to the best of your ability through continually transforming the dimensions within yourself (as led of the Lord), you are ready to unite with other people who are doing the same. This is basically the model for Group Ascension in Christ; and it is portrayed in the Book of Ezekiel.

Ascending corporately is quite different than ascending by yourself. Believers still legally ascend by the Holy Spirit through the cross and the blood to be "in Christ" – the *Alef/Tav*. The difference between ascending individually and corporately is like the difference between playing basketball by yourself, simply shooting hoops, or playing as a team. It's a difference ball game, and it can take some practice to learn to work together.

After taking on communion with the Father, the Son, the

Holy Spirit and myself the first time, I was told: Look to the Living Creature for the Order of Melchizedek. The Living Creature can also be called the Living Being, or the Cherubim. Sometimes I like to call the corporate Living Creature Formation of the Order of Melchizedek, the Cherubim Classification of the Order of Melchizedek. Notice Ezekiel 10 connects the two by telling us: *"THIS IS THE LIVING CREATURE that I saw under the God of Israel by the river of Chebar; and I knew that THEY WERE THE CHERUBIM" (Ezekiel 10.20 KJV).*

When the Father, the Son, the Holy Spirit and yourself unite in a fourfold way, that's an Order of Melchizedek position, even though in this instance I called them the Four Faces of God. When four or more people endeavor to fire on all these cylinders together, as they each unite with the Father, the Son, and Holy Spirit, the *Merkabah* of Ezekiel fame is formed. Notice: *"Out of the midst thereof came the likeness of FOUR LIVING CREATURES. And this was their appearance; they had the likeness of a man" (Ezekiel 1.5 KJV).* The "one man" in Ezekiel 1.5 is connected to the "One New Man in Christ" in Ephesians 2.15. Now connect this also to Metatron in its fullness…

Let's get the ascension picture here that's portrayed in the *Merkabah.* When the living creatures lift up from the earth, they are lifted up by the spirit of the One New Man in Christ. Notice the "lifted up" ascension language related to the four living creatures, the Living Creature, or the Cherubim in Scripture:

- *"When the living creatures were LIFTED UP from the earth [descension], the wheels were LIFTED UP. Whithersoever the spirit was to go, they went, thither their spirit to go: and the wheels were LIFTED UP over against them: for the spirit of the Living Creature was in the wheels. When those went, these went; and when those stood, these stood; and when those were LIFTED UP from the earth, the wheels were LIFTED UP over against them: for the spirit of the Living Creature was in the wheels"* (Ezekiel 1.19-21 KJV).

- *"And every one had four faces: the first face was the face of a cherub, and the second face was the face of a man, and the third face of a lion, and the fourth the face of an eagle. And the Cherubim were LIFTED UP. This is the Living Creature that I saw by the river Chebar. And when the Cherubim went, the wheels went by them: and when the Cherubim LIFTED UP their wings to mount up from the earth, the same wheels also turned not from beside them. When they stood, these stood; and when they were LIFTED UP, these LIFTED UP themselves also: for the spirit of the Living Creature was in them"* (Ezekiel 10.14-17 KJV).

In group ascensions, we should first look up in the Spirit, as one, to connect vertically to the One who sits on the Throne and unto the Lamb, which causes each one of us to be "in Christ" with a protective coating of His blood; and then, we look horizontally in the Spirit to connect to one another. This is how a group of people can manifestly be quickened together with Christ where they are raised up together and seated together in heavenly places in Christ

(Ephesians 2.5-6).

The Living Creature Formation of the Order of
Melchizedek moves according to the spirit of the Corporate
Living Creature, which moves according to the Holy Spirit
of the Living God. Each person who participates in a
Group Ascension is pictured in Ezekiel as one of the living
creatures with one wheel upon the earth with his four faces:
*"Now as I beheld the living creatures, behold one wheel upon the earth
by the living creatures, with his four faces"* (*Ezekiel 1.15* KJV).

Even though every person in a corporate ascension is
actually ascending and descending separately, the group's
unified desire to do only what we see the Father doing
(John 5.19) causes them to operate as a unified whole –
One New Man in Christ. Please notice the ascension
language in verse 19-20 of Ezekiel 1 marks the transition
from the plurality of four lifted-up "living creatures" to the
singularity of one ascended "Living Creature." This is when
four or more individuals in a Group Ascension truly
become unified as one in Christ, just as Jesus and the
Father are one.

Let me leave you with one last thought: When man (i.e.,
Israel) sinned, the face of the ox (representative of the
Father) was replaced with the cherub, which is why priests
of the Order of Melchizedek have to descend and ascend
to re-establish the Face of the Ox in their own life… as
well as descending and ascending corporately.

The counterfeit Metatron is called Meta-tron Mithra, which

is connected to Christmas, where society and most of the church have twisted the righteous reality of the fullness of the Messiah. God's personal and intimate friends cannot become part of the full manifestation of the One New Man in Christ – Metatron – if we celebrate Christmas. That is one of my life's messages to the Body of Christ as part of His Bride. The counterfeit Metatron is Meta-tron Mithra, the archangel (i.e., fallen archangel), a divine charioteer that ushers worshippers into the presence of the sun god [to have spiritual experiences through mystic rites].

You and I are meant to ride the *Merkabah* ultimately as an integral part of eternal and true Metatron (Messiah). Do you want a cheap counterfeit or the righteous real? Please follow Jesus's pattern by descending to the dimension(s) within yourself that love Christmas and look for Yeshua and Y-H-V-H there. Ask what He thinks. Look at Scripture. Examine if you truly reflect His purity and truth.

The thirteen "I AM" Statement that Yeshua proclaimed during the Feast of Dedication (dedication of one's heart) says this: *"Jesus said to them, 'Is it not so written in your law, I said, you are gods? If he called them gods because the Word of God was with them* [fullness of the ORDER of Melchizedek] *(and Scripture cannot be broken). Why to the one whom the Father sanctified and sent to the world, do you say, You blaspheme, just because I said to you, I AM THE SON OF GOD'"* (John 10.34-36 *Aramaic*). Melchizedek is made like unto the Son of God. The Metatron Merkabah Army is made like unto the Son of God in His fullness.

7 – 144,000 FIRSTFRUIT

144,000 Virgin Company are a bridal company of people made up of spiritually pure people in His eyes. They are 144,000 people sealed from all the tribes of the children of Israel. Within these tribes, the people called to be part of the 144,000 cover the broadest spectrum of race, gender, creed, color, and blood. The 144,000 Virgin Bride all have Jewish blood in them from one drop to being full-blooded.

These 144,000 people with Jewish blood in them have been sealed for such a time as this. They are merely the *"firstfruits unto God and to the Lamb"* of a great bridal company of people who *"follow the Lamb wherever He goes" (Revelation 14.4)*.

The winds that have been held back for the sealing of the 144,000 are now beginning to blow. The four winds are blowing these 144,000 leaves for the healing of the nations. The four winds and the angels are blowing the Joel 2 Trumpet, which will release His Metatron Merkabah

(Melchizedek) Army.

¹ And after these things I saw FOUR ANGELS standing on the four corners of the earth, holding the FOUR WINDS of the earth, that the wind should not blow on the earth, nor on the sea, nor on any tree. ² And I saw another angel ascending from the east, having the seal of the living God: and he cried with a loud voice to the four angels, to whom it was given to hurt the earth and the sea. ³ Saying, Hurt not the earth, neither the sea, nor the trees, till we have sealed the servants of our God in their foreheads. ⁴ And I heard the number of them which were sealed: and there were sealed a HUNDRED AND FORTY AND FOUR THOUSAND OF ALL THE TRIBES OF THE CHILDREN OF ISRAEL [Virgin Bride]. ⁵ Of the tribe of Judah were sealed twelve thousand. Of the tribe of Reuben were sealed twelve thousand. Of the tribe of Gad were sealed twelve thousand. ⁶ Of the tribe of Asher were sealed twelve thousand. Of the tribe of Naphtali were sealed twelve thousand. Of the tribe of Manasseh were sealed twelve thousand. ⁷ Of the tribe of Simeon were sealed twelve thousand. Of the tribe of Levi were sealed twelve thousand. Of the tribe of Issachar were sealed twelve thousand. ⁸ Of the tribe of Zebulun were sealed twelve thousand. Of the tribe of Joseph were sealed twelve thousand. Of the tribe of Benjamin were sealed twelve thousand (Revelation 7.1-8 KJV).

The first half of Revelation 7 (verses 1-8) has probably been the most abused passage in the Bible, which reveals the sealing of 144,000 Jewish bond-servants of God. Many cults, including the Jehovah Witnesses, falsely claim they are the fulfillment of the 144,000. Most mainline Christians believe that the 144,000 is symbolic of the Church.

Revelation 7.1-8 specifies they are 144,000 Jews and enumerates them by their tribes.

Notice that this list starts with Tribe of Judah (earthly lineage of Yeshua - Jesus) and ends with the Tribe of Benjamin. The Tribe of Benjamin was among the Tribe of Judah, because Jerusalem was between the two of them. Therefore, we need to understand that the Tribe of Benjamin is included with the Tribe of Judah as detailed in *1 Kings 12.20-21: "²⁰ Now it came to pass when all Israel heard Jeroboam had come back, they sent for him and called him to the congregation, and made him king over all Israel. There was none who followed the house of David, but the Tribe of Judah only. ²¹And when Rehoboam came to Jerusalem, he assembled all the House of Judah with the Tribe of Benjamin, one hundred and eighty thousand chosen men..." (1 Kings 12.20-21a* NKJV). The Tribe of Judah and the Tribe of Benjamin are two bookends (i.e., paw prints of the lion) that speaks of One Tribe – the sons of His right hand whose language is praise.

The Tribe of Judah and the Tribe of Benjamin were also among those who spoke blessings from Mount Gerizim (Mount of Blessings) just prior to the nation of Israel crossing the Jordan into the Promised Land: *"⁹And Moses and the priests and the Levites said to all Israel, Give ear and harken, O Israel; this day you have become the people of the LORD your God. ¹⁰ You shall therefore obey the voice of the Lord your God, and do His commandments and His statutes which I command you this day. ¹¹ And Moses charged the people that same day, saying, ¹² these tribes shall stand upon Mount Gerizim to bless the people when* *you have crossed the Jordan: Simeon, Levi, Judah, Issachar, Joseph and Benjamin. ¹³ And these tribes shall stand upon Gebel to curse: Reuben, Gad, Asher, Zebulun, Dan, and Naphtali" (Deuteronomy 27.9-13 _{Aramaic}).*

Notice that the list of the 144,000 in Revelation 7 does not include the original Tribe of Dan, but the Tribe of Manasseh. Ephraim and Manasseh make up the House of Joseph; therefore, the House of Joseph has a special and unique double portion in the 144,000 with the tribe of Joseph and Manasseh included.

The original 12 tribes include both the tribes of Levi and Joseph, but Levi (the priestly tribe) is not usually listed because its inheritance is the Lord Himself (Deuteronomy 10.9). Additionally, Joseph's name is usually dropped and replaced by his two sons – Ephraim and Manasseh – who were adopted by Jacob (Genesis 48.8-22). Therefore, in the list of the 12 tribes of Israel, Levi and Joseph are typically replaced by Ephraim and Manasseh. However, in the tribal listing in Revelation 7, the tribes of Dan and Ephraim have been dropped and replaced by Levi and Joseph, keeping the list to 12. My guess as to why the tribes of Dan and Ephraim were removed from this 144,000 Virgin Bride list is that they were the ones who led the children of Israel into idolatry (1 Kings 12.25-30), which is one of the works of the flesh where those who do such things shall not inherit the Kingdom of God (1 Corinthians 6.9-10; Galatians 5.19-21).

Additionally, when the Promise Land was divided among the 12 tribes after the exodus from Egypt, Dan received his portion in the very north – the north gate: *"The spirit lifted me up between the earth and the heaven, and brought me in the visions of God to Jerusalem, to the door of the inner gate that looks toward the north; where was the seat of the image of jealousy, which provokes to jealously"* (*Ezekiel 8.3*). Check out Judges 18. According to Dan's name, the north gate is the gate of judgment.

12,000 from the Tribe of Judah were sealed

12,000 from the Tribe of Reuben were sealed

12,000 from the Tribe of Gad were sealed

12,000 from the Tribe of Asher were sealed

12,000 from the Tribe of Naphtali were sealed

12,000 from the Tribe of Manasseh were sealed

12,000 from the Tribe of Simeon were sealed

12,000 from the Tribe of Levi were sealed

12,000 from the Tribe of Issachar were sealed

12,000 from the Tribe of Zebulun were sealed

12,000 from the Tribe of Joseph were sealed

12,000 from the Tribe of Benjamin were sealed

144,000 sealed from all the tribes of the children of Israel (Revelation 7:4). The word "sealed" is mentioned 15 times in Revelation 7. It is the Greek word *sphragizo* (sfrag-id'-zo) - Strong's NT:4972. This Revelation 7 seal is obviously some type of stamp or impression that marks the authenticity of these 144,000 Hebrew souls. The Greek definition of this seal includes the idea that the seal is for security purposes or preservation as well as implying keeping something secret. It is also the guarantee of God that attests to the genuineness of the 144,000 Virgin Bride. It authenticates the witness of the 144,000 Hebrew souls as true. This seal (according to Revelation 14.1) is the name of the Lamb's Father written on their brows.

"And I heard the number of those who were sealed; and it was a hundred and forty and four thousand of ALL the tribes of the children of Israel" (Revelation 7.4 ₐᵣₐₘₐᵢ꜀). How can this be? The Tribe of Dan is missing from the 144,000 list in Revelation 7, yet it says *"144,000 from ALL the tribes of the children of Israel," (Revelation 7:4).* The Lord told me that He has caused the Danites to marry into the other tribes. Even though they will not have representatives of the Tribe of Dan as part of the 144,000, they will be married to ones that are.

" ¹And I looked, and, lo, the Lamb stood on Mount Zion, and with Him a hundred and forty-four thousand in number, having the name of His Father written in their brows. ² Then I heard a voice from heaven, like the sound of many waters and like the sound of a great thunder; and the voice I heard was like the music of many harpists playing on their harps; ³And they sang a new song before the throne and before the four animals and the elders; and no man was able to

learn that song except the hundred and forty-four thousand who were redeemed from the earth. [4] *These are those who were not defiled with women, for they are pure. These are those who follow the Lamb wherever He goes. These were redeemed by Jesus from among men to be the first fruits to God and to the Lamb.* [5] *And in their mouth was found no deceit; for they are without fault"* (Revelation 14.1-5 _{Aramaic}).

Revelation 14.4 is a key to the 144,000. Let's break down this verse:

[1] *"These are those who were not defiled with women, for they are pure..."* (Revelation 14.4a).

1. "The 144,000 Virgin Company are a bridal company of people made up of spiritually pure people in His eyes. They are 144,000 people sealed from all the tribes of the children of Israel. Within these tribes, the people called to be part of the 144,000 cover the broadest spectrum of race, gender and blood. The 144,000 Bride all have Jewish blood in them from one drop to being full-blooded." Why I can confidently say this is because I received a personal and epiphaneous appearance from Yeshua and the Archangel Gabriel on December 4, 1999 in Colorado Springs. One of the things downloaded into my brain from a beam of light plugged into the top of my head was about the 144,000 Virgin Bride who will cover the broadest spectrum within the confines of representing all the tribes of Israel.

2. Additionally, we can study the text:

a. <u>BROADEST SPECTRUM OF PEOPLE</u>: *"These are they which are not defiled with women for they are virgins" (Revelation 14.4 KJV)*. "These" in the phrase "These are they" is the Greek word *houtos* [NT:3778]. It is the most frequently used pronoun in Scripture that can mean either he, she, or it. It literally points to a person within all persons, genders and numbers (i.e., mankind). You will be hard-pressed to find a more broad pronoun than *houtos*. That's why I say: The 144,000 Virgin Bride will cover the broadest spectrum within the confines of representing all the tribes of Israel.

b. <u>SPIRITUALLY PURE</u>: *"These are they which are not defiled with women for they are virgins."* The word "defiled" here is used in the New Testament of those who have not kept themselves pure from the defilement of sin, who have soiled themselves by fornication and adultery.

" 15 Do you not know that your bodies are the members of Christ? How then can one take a member of Christ and make it the member of a harlot? Far be it. 16 Or do you not know that he who joins his body to a harlot is one body with her? For it is said, The two shall become one body. 17 But he who unites himself with our Lord becomes one with him in spirit. 18 Keep away from FORNICATION. Every sin that a man commits is outside his body; but he who commits ADULTERY sins against his own body. 19 Or do you not

know that your body is the temple of the Holy Spirit that dwells within you, which you have of God, and you are not your own? [20] *For you have been <u>bought with a price</u>; therefore glorify God in your body and in your spirit, because they belong to God" (1 Corinthians 6.15-20* Aramaic*).*

This goes with the context that follows Revelation 14.1-5: *"* [6] *And I saw another angel fly in the midst of heaven, having the everlasting gospel to preach unto them that dwell on the earth, and to every nation, and kindred, and tongue, and people,* [7] *saying with a loud voice, Fear God, and give glory to Him; for the hour of His judgment is come: and worship Him that made heaven and earth, and the sea, and the fountains of waters.* [8] *And there followed another angel, saying, Babylon is fallen, is fallen, that great city, because she made all nations drink of the wine of the wrath of her FORNICATION.* [9] *And the third angel followed them, saying with a loud voice, If any man worship the beast and his image, and receive his mark in his forehead, or in his hand.* [10] *The same shall drink of the wine of the wrath of God, which is poured out without mixture into the cup of His indignation; and He shall be tormented with fire and brimstone in the presence of the holy angels, and in the presence of the Lamb:* [11] *And the smoke of their torment ascends up for ever and ever: and they have no rest day nor night, who worship the beast and his image, and whosoever receives the mark of his name.* [12] *Here is the patience of the saints: here are they that keep the commandments of God, and the faith of Jesus" (Revelation 14.6-12* KJV*).*

<u>BABYLON</u>: *"Babylon is fallen, is fallen, that great city, because she made all nations drink of the wine of the wrath of her FORNICATION" (Revelation 14.8 KJV):*

1) *" ² Babylon the great is fallen, is fallen. And is become the habitation of devils, and the hold of every foul spirit, and a cage of every unclean and hateful bird. ³ For all nations have drunk of the wine of the wrath of her FORNICATION, and the kings of the earth have committed FORNICATION with her, and the merchants of the earth are waxed rich through the abundance of her delicacies" (Revelation 18.2-3 KJV).*

2) *" ¹ Come hither; I will show unto thee the judgment of the GREAT WHORE that sits upon many water; ² With whom the kings of the earth have committed FORNICATION, and the inhabitants of the earth have been made drunk with the wine of her FORNICATION … ⁵ And upon her forehead was a name written, MYSTERY, BABYLON THE GREAT, THE MOTHER OF HARLOTS AND ABOMINATIONS OF THE EARTH"* (Revelation 17.1-2,5 KJV).

    a. *"These are they which are not defiled with women for they are virgins."* Therefore, these "virgins" can either mean a marriageable maiden or young bride, or a man/woman who has abstained from all uncleanness and whoredom associated with idolatry.

2 Corinthians 11.2 puts it this way. Paul says: *"2 For I am zealous for you with the zealousness of God, for I have espoused you to a husband, that I may PRESENT YOU AS A PURE VIRGIN TO CHRIST. 3 But I am afraid that just as the serpent through his deceitfulness misled Eve, so your minds should be corrupted from the sincerity that is in Christ"* (2 Corinthians 11.2-3 *Aramaic*).

[2] *"These are those who follow the Lamb wherever He goes"* *(Revelation 14.4b).*

1. *"John [the Baptist] saw Jesus coming toward him, and said. 'Behold! The Lamb of God who takes away the sins of the world!"* *(John 1.29 NKJV).*

2. The only sacrifice that covers intentional sin is the Lamb of God Offering foreshadowed in Genesis 22.

3. *"6 And I beheld, and lo, in the midst of the elders, stood a Lamb as it had been slain, having seven horns and seven eyes, which are the seven Spirits of God sent forth into all the earth, 7 And He came and took the book from the right hand of him who sat upon the throne. 8 And as he took the book, the four animals and the four and twenty elders fell down before the Lamb, and everyone of them had a harp and a cup of gold full of incense, and these were the prayers of the saints. 9 And they sang new praise saying, Thou are worthy to take the book and to open the seals thereof; for thou was*

slain and has redeemed us to God by thy blood out of every tribe and tongue and people and nation: ¹⁰And has made them for our God kings and priests; and they shall reign on the earth. ¹¹And I looked, and I heard as it were the voice of many angels round about the throne and the animals and the elders; and their number was ten thousand times ten thousand, and thousands of thousands, ¹²saying with a loud voice, WORTHY IS THE LAMB THAT WAS SLAIN TO RECEIVE POWER AND RICHES AND WISDOM AND MIGHT AND HONOR AND GLORY AND BLESSING. ¹³And every creature which is on heaven and on the earth and under the earth and all that are in the sea and all that are in them. I heard saying, To Him who sits on the throne and TO THE LAMB BE BLESSING AND HONOR AND GLORY AND DOMINION for ever and ever" (Revelation 5.8-13 ₐᵣₐₘₐᵢ꜀).

4. The 144,000 are simply the first fruits of those who follow the Lamb wherever He goes. Listen to this Revelation 7 passage right after the 144,000 are sealed: *"⁹ After these things I beheld, and lo, a great multitude which no man could number, of EVERY NATION AND PEOPLE AND KINDRED AND TONGUE STOOD BEFORE THE THRONE AND IN THE PRESENCE OF THE LAMB, clothed with white robes and with palms in their hands, ¹⁰And cried with a loud voice, saying, Salvation to our God, who sits upon the throne, and to the Lamb. ¹¹And all the angels stood round about the throne and about the*

elders and the four animals, and fell before His throne on their faces, and worshipped God, [12] *saying, Amen! Blessing and glory and wisdom and thanksgiving and honor and power and might to our God for ever and ever. Amen.* [13] *And one of the elders answered, saying to me, Who are these who are arrayed in white robes? And from whence did they come?* [14] *And I said to him, My lord, you know. And he said to me, THESE ARE THOSE WHO CAME OUT OF THE GREAT TRIBULATION, AND HAVE WASHED THEIR ROBES AND MADE THEM WHITE IN THE BLOOD OF THE LAMB.* [15] *Therefore they are before the throne of God, and serve Him day and night in His Temple; and He who sits on the Throne shall shelter them.* [16] *They shall hunger no more, neither thirst anymore; neither shall they be stricken by the sun not by the heat.* [17] *FOR THE LAMB WHO IS IN THE MIDST OF THE THRONE SHALL SHEPHERD THEM AND SHALL LEAD THEM TO FOUNTAINS OF LIVING WATER. And God shall wipe away all tears from their eyes"* (Revelation 14.9-17 Aramaic).

[3] *"They were redeemed by Jesus from among men"* (Revelation 14.4c).

1. Let's look at the phrase *"Redeemed by Jesus from among men."* The term *"among men"* includes all of humanity. Its Greek root means "man-faced," which focuses on looking at or beholding. This concept of man-faced redemption by Jesus includes

the concept that the real person is being seen.

2. The term *"were redeemed"* is the Greek word *agorazo* [Strong's NT:59], which is defined to be: (1) to go to market, (2) to do business (buy or sell), or (3) to purchase.

> *"FOR YOU ARE BOUGHT WITH A PRICE; therefore glorify God in body, in your spirit, which are God's" (1 Corinthians 6.20).*

3. *"And they* [four living creatures and twenty-four elders] *sang a new song, saying: 'You are worthy to take the scroll, and to open its seals; for You were slain, and HAVE REDEEMED US TO GOD BY YOUR BLOOD out of every tribe and tongue and people and nation" (Revelation 5.9).*

4. The ten virgins had to purchase (buy) oil for themselves in order to be ready to meet the Bridegroom and the 144,000 Virgin Bride: *"¹ Then the Kingdom of Heaven will be like Ten Virgins, who took their lamps and went out to greet the bridegroom and the bride. ² Five of them were wise, and five were foolish. ³ And the foolish ones took their lamps, but took no oil with them. ⁴ But the wise ones took oil in the vessels with their lamps. ⁵As the bridegroom was delayed, they all slumbered and slept. ⁶And at midnight there was a cry. Behold, the bridegroom is coming is coming; go out to greet him!⁷ Then all the virgins got up and prepared their lamps. ⁸And the foolish ones said to the wise ones, Give us some of your oil,*

for our lamps are going out. [9] Then the wise ones answered, saying, Why, there would not be enough for us and for you; GO TO THOSE WHO SELL AND BUY FOR YOURSELVES. [10] AND WHILE THEY WENT TO BUY, THE BRIDEGROOM CAME; and those who were ready entered with Him into the banqueting house, and the door was locked. [11] Afterward the other virgins also came and said, Our lord, our lord. Open to us. [12] But He answered and said to them, Truly I say to you, I do not know you" (Matthew 25.1-12 Aramaic).

5.   A merchant man sold all he had in order to buy the Pearl of Great Price, which the Kingdom of Heaven is likened to (Matthew 13.45-46).

[4]   *"To be first fruits to God and to the Lamb"* (Revelation 14.4d).

1.   <u>SEPARATION AND BEING THE FIRST</u>: The Greek word for "first fruits" is Strong's NT:536 *aparche*, which is a compound word made up of Strong's NT:575 *apo* and NT:756 *archomai*.

Apo signifies separation. In particular, it is a separation of a part from the whole.

Archomai communicates being the first to do (anything), to begin, to commence (in order of time).

Mysteries of the 144,000 Firstfruits

The 144,000 Virgin Bride are *"the firstfruits unto God and to the Lamb"* who will be separated (taken by God) from the whole of humanity. These 144,000 Firstfruits have been consecrated to God for all time. They will be simply the first to commence (in time) being taken up by God, like Enoch, for the purpose of God replacing their mortality with immortality (amongst other things). Never forget that others will follow these 144,000 *"firstfruits unto God and to the Lamb."*

Like Enoch (the forerunner of these 144,000 Firstfruits), they are pious worshippers of God who will be removed from the dwellers on earth and raised up to heaven where they will receive the name (office) of Metatron. Second Enoch 22 shows us that Enoch was transformed into an angel, resurrected, and then sent back to earth. Angels took up Enoch body, soul and spirit on their wings to the tenth heaven called Araboth where Enoch sees the LORD's throne and face. This is the place where Enoch's mortality (i.e., "his earthly clothing") was replaced with immortality (i.e., "put him into My splendid clothing"). Enoch's carnal body changed into one of light.

<u>2 Enoch 22</u>: *"On the tenth heaven, which is called Araboth, I saw the appearance of the Lord's face. The Lord's face was like an iron made to glow in fire, and brought out, emitting sparks, and burning. Thus in a moment of eternity I saw the Lord's face, but the Lord's face is inexpressible, spectacular and very dreadful, and very, very terrible.*

Who am I to tell of the Lord's unspeakable being, and of His very astonishing face? I cannot tell of the quality of His many instructions, and various voices! The Lord's throne is very impressive and not made with hands! I cannot tell of the quality of those standing round Him, the troops of cherubim and seraphim, nor their constant singing, nor His indisputable beauty, and who shall tell of the inexpressible greatness of His splendor!

I fell prone and bowed down to the Lord, and the Lord said to me with His lips, 'Take heart, Enoch! Don't be afraid! Arise and stand in My Presence into eternity!'

The chief general Michael lifted me up, and led me to the Lord's Presence. The Lord said to His servants, persuading them, 'Let Enoch stand in My Presence into eternity!'

The splendid ones bowed down to the Lord and said, 'Let Enoch go according to Your command.'

The Lord said to Michael, 'Go and take Enoch out of his earthly clothing [mortality]*, and anoint him with My sweet ointment, and put him into My splendid clothing* [immortality]. *'*

Michael did as the Lord told him. He anointed me, and dressed me. The appearance of that ointment is stronger than the great light, and is like sweet dew, and has a gentle fragrance, and shines like the sun's ray. I looked at myself, and I was like one of His splendid ones."

Enoch was transformed into an angel, resurrected, and sent back to earth. The Book of Second Enoch chapter 22 reveals Enoch as a High Priest who ascended to heaven to stand before the Throne of God. There the LORD summons the Archangel Michael to remove Enoch's earthly clothing (his mortal body) and to dress him in the garments of glory, which was his resurrected body. In the language of the Heavenly Temple, resurrection was/is a *theosis* – transformation of a human being into a divine being, not a post-mortem experience. After Michael dressed Enoch in garments of glory, Enoch was anointed with fragrant myrrh oil and Enoch saw himself transform into an angel. The second Book of Enoch chapter 22 tells us that the LORD said to Archangel Michael: *"Go and take Enoch from his earthly clothing"* [corrupted fallen mortal body]. And so Michael did just as the LORD commanded him. He anointed Enoch and he clothed Enoch in the splendid clothing of immortality. The myrrh oil that anointed Enoch came from the Tree of Life. The appearance of the myrrh oil was/is greater than the greatest light, and its ointment is like sweet dew [symbol of resurrection] and its fragrance is myrrh, and it is like the rays of the glittering sun. When Enoch looked at his reflection, he saw that he had become like one of the glorious ones. Then immediately, Enoch began to see the six days of creation after this.

Let's look closer at some key "first fruits" Scriptures, because the 144,000 Virgin Bride *"redeemed from the earth" (Rev 14.3)… "redeemed from among men" (Rev 14.4)* **are a particular type of FIRST FRUIT, which is connected to Enoch and resurrection life:**

[1]   **First, never forget that the 144,000 are all from the tribes of the children of Israel.** Every single

person in the 144,000 have Jewish blood in them. These 144,000 Hebrews (ones who have crossed over) are a remnant according to the election of grace (Romans 11:5), which is the fullness of the children of Israel (Romans 11:12). The receiving of the 144,000 Virgin Bride in heaven, when God takes them, will bring forth resurrection life (Romans 11:15). Just as the first fruits of the 144,000 Virgin Bride is holy, so will be those who prepare themselves as wise virgins (Romans 11:16):

"⁵ Even so then at this present time also there is a remnant according to the election of grace …¹² Now if the fall of them be riches of the world, and the diminishing of them the riches of the Gentiles; how much more their fullness? ¹³ For I speak to you Gentiles, inasmuch as I am the apostle of the Gentiles, I magnify mine office: ¹⁴ If by any means I may provoke to emulation them which are my flesh, and might save some of them. ¹⁵ For if the casting away of them be the reconciling of the world, what shall the receiving of them be, but life from the dead [resurrection life]*? ¹⁶ FOR IF THE FIRSTFRUITS BE HOLY, THE LUMP IS ALSO HOLY: and if the root be holy, so are the branches" (Romans 11.5, 12-16* KJV*).*

REMEMBER THE 144,000 FIRSTFRUITS ARE CONSIDERED TO BE HOLY IN GOD'S EYES. Just as the first portion of the dough is considered holy for the sacred loaves, so are the 144,000. *'The cup of blessing which we bless, is it not the*

159

communion of the blood of Christ? The bread which we break, is it not the communion of the body of Christ? For we being many are one bread, and one body: for we are all partakers of that bread" (1 Corinthians 10:16-17 KJV)

[2]   **The 144,000 Hebrew souls have all received the FIRST FRUITS OF THE SPIRIT to be in Christ in order to manifest the redemption of their bodies:**

" 19 For the earnest expectation of the creature waits for the manifestation of the sons of God. 20 For the creature was made subject to vanity, not willingly, but by reason of him who has subjected the same in hope; 21 because the creature itself also shall be delivered from the bondage of corruption into the glorious liberty of the children of God. 22 For we know that the whole creation groans and travails in pain together until now. 23 And not only they, but ourselves also, which have THE FIRSTFRUITS OF THE SPIRIT, even we ourselves groan within ourselves, waiting for the adoption, to wit, THE REDEMPTION OF OUR BODY" (Romans 8:19-23 KJV).

[3]   **The 144,000 Hebrew souls follow the Pattern Son – the Lamb of God – wherever He goes. In Christ they shall all be made alive according to resurrection life.**

160

When we read this passage in 1 Corinthians 15, let's consider another dimension to *"them that sleep" (1 Corinthians 15.20)* and *"for the trumpet shall sound, and the dead shall be raised incorruptible, and we shall be changed" (1 Corinthians 15.52)*.

"Them that sleep" (1 Cor 15.20) ... "We shall not all sleep, but we shall all be changed" (1 Cor 15.51) - Consider that Enoch was taken and returned body, soul and spirit while he was asleep on earth. His son Methuselah knew approximately when Enoch would return and where, because *"Methuselah had been expecting my coming and had kept watch night and day at my bed. He was filled with awe when he heard my coming" (2 Enoch 38)*.

"For the trumpet shall sound, and the dead shall be raised incorruptible, and we shall be changed" (1 Corinthians 15.52) – What if *"the dead"* who are raised incorruptible are totally Crucified Ones where they are crucified in total union with Christ… where the life they live in the flesh, they live according to the exact same faith of the Son of God (Galatians 2:20). They are ready to perfectly unite with the mature head of the Messiah Yeshua as His fully mature Body… as Metatron… the undifferentiated state of the Messiah – the fullness of the heavenly One New Man in Christ.

" [21] For since by man came death, by man came also the resurrection of the dead. [22] For as in Adam all die, even so IN

CHRIST ALL BE MADE ALIVE. [23] *But every man in his own order: CHRIST THE FIRSTFRUITS; AFTERWARD THEY THAT ARE CHRIST'S AT HIS COMING.* [24] *Then comes the end, when He shall have delivered up the Kingdom of God, even the Father; when He shall put down all rule, and all authority and power. ...* [42] *So also is the resurrection of the dead. It is sown in corruption, it is raised in incorruption:* [43] *It is sown in dishonor, it is raised in glory: it is sown in corruption, it is raised in incorruption:* [44] *It is sown a natural body, it is raised a spiritual body. There is a natural body, and there is a spiritual body.* [45] *And so it is written, The first man Adam was made a living soul; the last Adam was made a quickening spirit.* [46] *Howbeit that was not first which is spiritual, but that which is natural; and afterward that which is spiritual.* [47] *The first man is of the earth, earthly; the second man is the Lord from heaven.* [48] *As is the earthly, such are they also that are earthly: and as is the heavenly, such are they also that are heavenly.* [49] *And as we have borne the image of the earthly, we shall also bear the image of the heavenly.* [50] *Now this I say, brethren, that flesh and blood cannot inherit the Kingdom of God; neither does corruption inherit incorruption.* [51] *Behold, I show you a mystery; We shall not all sleep, but we shall all be changed.* [52] *In a moment, in the twinkling of an eye, at the last trump:* FOR THE TRUMPET SHALL SOUND, AND THE DEAD [TOTALLY CRUCIFIED ONES] SHALL BE RAISED INCORRUPTIBLE, AND WE SHALL BE CHANGED. [53] FOR THIS CORRUPTION MUST PUT ON INCORRUPTION, AND THIS MORTAL MUST PUT ON

IMMORTALITY. *⁵⁴ So when this corruption shall have put on incorruption, and this mortal shall have put on immortality, then shall be brought to pass the saying that is written, Death is swallowed up in victory"* (1 Corinthians 15.21-24, 42-54 ₖⱼᵥ).

*****

New Jerusalem

The wall of the New Jerusalem 144 cubits (Revelation 21:17).

144 cube it is.

The New Jerusalem's walls are 144 cubits (215 feet thick).

Also know that in sacred geometry, a cube is a platonic solid. It is symbolic of the earth (i.e., space time).

*"¹And **I saw a new heaven and a new earth**: for the first heaven and the first earth were passed away; and there were no more sea. ²And I John saw **the holy city, New Jerusalem, coming down from God out of heaven, prepared as a bride adorned for her husband**. ³And I heard a great voice out of heaven saying, Behold, the tabernacle of God is with men, and He will dwell with them, and they shall be His people, and God Himself shall be with them, and be their God. ⁴And God shall wipe away all tears from their eyes; and there shall be no more death, neither sorrow, nor crying, neither shall there be any more pain: for the former things*

are passed away. *⁵And he that sat upon the throne said, Behold, I make all things new. And he said unto me, Write: for these words are true and faithful. ⁶And he said unto me, It is done. I am Alpha and Omega, the beginning and the end. I will give unto him that is athirst of the fountain of the water of life freely. ⁷ He that overcometh shall inherit all things; and I will be his God, and he shall be My son. ⁸ But the fearful, and unbelieving, and the abominable, and murderers, and whoremongers, and sorcerers, and idolaters, and all liars, shall have their part in the lake which burneth with fire and brimstone: which is the second death. ⁹And there came unto me one of the seven angels which had the seven vials full of the seven last plagues, and talked with me, saying, **Come hither, I will show thee the Bride, the Lamb's wife.** ¹⁰And He carried me away in the spirit to a great and high mountain, and showed me that great city, the holy Jerusalem, descending out of heaven from God. ¹¹ Having the glory of God: and her light was like unto a stone most precious, even like a jasper stone, clear as crystal; ¹²And had a wall great and high, and had **twelve gates, and at the gates twelve angels, and names written thereon, which are the names of the twelve tribes of the children of Israel**: ¹³ On the east three gates; on the north three gates; on the south three gates; and on the west three gates. ¹⁴ And the wall of the city had twelve foundations, and in them the names of the twelve apostles of the Lamb. ¹⁵ And he that talked with me had a golden reed to measure the city, and the gates thereof, and the wall thereof. ¹⁶And the city lies foursquare, and the length is as large as the breadth: and **he measured the city with the reed, 12,000 furlongs. The length and the breadth and the height of it are equal.** ¹⁷And he measured **the wall** thereof **144 cubits**, according to the measure of man, that is, of the *angel. [18]And the building of the wall of it was of jasper: and the city was pure gold, like unto clear glass. [19]And the foundation of the wall of the city were garnished with all manner of precious stones. The first foundation was jasper; the second sapphire; the third, a chalcedony; the fourth, an emerald; [20] The fifth, saradonyx; the sixth, sardius; the seventh, chrysolite; the eighth, beryl; the ninth, a topaz; the tenth, a chrysoprasus; the eleventh, a jacinth; the twelfth, an amethyst. [21]And* **the twelve gates were twelve pearls; every several gate was of one pearl***: and the street of the city was pure gold, as it were transparent glass. [22]And I saw no temple therein: for the Lord God Almighty and the Lamb are the temple in it. [23]And the city had no need of the sun, neither the moon, to shine in it: for the glory of God did lighten it, and the Lamb is the light thereof. [24]And the nations of them which are saved shall walk in the light of it: and the kings of the earth do bring their glory and honor into it. [25]And the gates of it shall not be shut at all by day: for there shall be no night there. [26]And they shall bring the glory and honor of the nations into it. [27]And there shall be in no wise enter into it any thing that defiles, neither whatsoever works abomination, or makes a lie: but they which are written in the Lamb's Book of Life" (Revelation 21.1-27 KJV).*

Notice how Revelation 21.1 speaks of a new heaven and a new earth before Revelation 21.2 shows us the crystal-clear golden cube of the New Jerusalem descending out of heaven from God.

"[13] Nevertheless we, according to His promise, look for new heavens and a new earth, wherein dwells righteousness. [14] Wherefore, beloved, seeing that you look for such things, be diligent that you may be found of Him in peace, without spot, and blameless" (2 Peter 3.13-14).

This makes sense, because as Revelation 21.9 tells us, the New Jerusalem is the wife of the Lamb, and Revelation 19.7-8 reveals that His Bride is clothed in bright, clean, fine linen, which is the righteous deeds/acts of the saints. We are living in the glorious day when the pure and spotless Virgin Bridal Company of the 144,000 is being revealed... transformed... transfigured... being first fruits of the resurrection of the body.

Remember how the Kingdom of Heaven is likened unto the Pearl of Great Price that needs to be purchased – bought - redeemed (Matt 13.45-46)?

The New Jerusalem has 12 gates of 12 pearls with the names of the 12 tribes of the children of Israel written on each of them. Know that the DNA of the fullness of each of the 12 tribes of the children of Israel (of the 144,000) is the combination to unlock the descending new heaven and new earth of the New Jerusalem.

1 furlong = 0.125 miles.

12,000 furlongs = 1500 miles.

Therefore, a 12,000 furlong cubic structure is 1500 miles length x 1500 miles width x 1500 miles height = 3,375,000,000 billion cubic miles

The City of God called the "New Jerusalem" in Revelation 21 is the size of a country where its height, length and width is the same – 12,000 furlongs according to the King James Version of the Bible.

*****

Many are receiving visions of the 144,000's soon departure. Many are receiving visions of warning.

I recommend two videos on YouTube that confirm a vision that a friend got:

[1] 144,000 ARE ABOUT TO LEAVE!!! DAYS OF DARKNESS IMMINENT! REPENT!! https://www.youtube.com/watch?v=XM3q0xHx7Gc

[2] PROPHETIC DREAM: "23 Degrees North" Departure Is At Hand – video by Paul Begley => https://www.youtube.com/watch?v=m8EN25SXj7Q [Note: Even though this interpretation is not technically incorrect due to all those who will follow the first fruits of the 144,000 Virgin Bride, it does leave out the common sense (most direct) interpretation that the 144,000 are all Hebrews from the twelve tribes of Israel listed in Revelation 7. Not only does Paul Begley leave out the step of the 144,000 Hebrews being taken by God, like Enoch, "the rapture" doctrine is also a bogus escaptology theory invented in 1830 by John Darby.]

A friend received the following vision on 10-24-2016: "I

went through to see and this is what I saw. It is long and I don't know if I can properly express it.

A beautiful day – the sky was clear – like beautiful water. Like people going about their normal day; but then, the judgment was stamped and an angel stirred up the waters – but when the water and wind increased, the Bride said – not so Lord. And mercy was shown for a moment… for a just a moment. Then I saw a brilliant flash of light. I relived passing the dump truck and found myself again on the table – hearing the song just as I died years ago… it's the end of the world. And there it was – the same brilliant light.

Then I flash to a short story I wrote, about a woman professor who was teaching her students about the mysteries of what was ancient and now being fulfilled. I watched as a principality grabbed the steering wheel of a delivery truck and forced the driver to hit the professor. Then there was a brilliant light as Watcher 7 showed me through its eyes what happened. But I knew that was only in a story I had written. Then I left that story and was back above and looked down upon the earth.

I saw the light appear in the north – 23 degrees. Yes – it was north at 23. Then I saw that many are being shown the vision – both a vision of warning and a vision of departure.

Then the earth was bathed in darkness, because the light was removed from the world because the waters of the deep churned as the light was removed – Matthew 24. I knew it was Hurricane Matthew and though the prayers had stayed God's hand, the light had been removed.

And then I was taken to see the future. Now, you know I am not a prophet, yet I saw. The earth was shaking violently, and the call was being shouted urgently to the Bride. The Bride who cried in the darkness: Prepare from above. Prepare from the Bride. And there was some who believed the trumpet call and put on clean clothes, even though the world was in darkness.

But it was not yet time to leave. So, the Bride gathered and listened to the voice – be patient. And there was fear on earth when the earth had stopped its shaking. There was silence in the darkness. And the Bride wonders: Is the Groom late? And the Bride wonders: Are we late? Were we not ready? But the voice said: Patience.

And a wind blew and a horn blew. Then there appeared yellow light… the entire atmosphere became yellow light – and it bathed the Bride so that the Bride became clothed in its yellow golden light. And I knew then a knowing for myself – and I ached with longing but said not my will Father – let Yours be done in me – because I saw and watched the Bride rising up – it was gone.

And there was confusion on earth – because only a remnant [144,000] were gone and not the church. Not even the children. And anger rose up in men's hearts – coldness of hearts among the church. And the trying of faith was begun.

As the Bride rose, they sang a new song – a song of joy, of

hope fulfilled – and the Bride rose up together with purpose. The Bride was not divided by race, dogma, or creed; but bonded in love of the King. As they rose up, there were others who were also gathering on the earth. They danced and sang and prayed and loved God and one another. They watched as the others rose up.

The gathered ones left behind grew strong, because their sinews were given strength by those who have left. They no longer needed to eat, but they provided much bread to the starving because the light had left the earth and the Bride had been taken up. Those who remained gathered in the 70 nations – who were the radiating light, like the skin of Adam was the Bride taken up and the nations radiated by reason of the skin of the Bride above them.

I heard again and I saw 23. Then I saw a circle – like the classes I have been teaching – every night I am taught of these things – but suddenly the need was so great and the time of darkness had arrived – and all the numbers and shapes and names flowed into me much more than before – as though in a few nights all I had learnt in a year of dreams was explained in much depth. Each flash having significance – each carrying with it the pattern and flow of the days coming after the quake – after the Bride had gone above – messages for those who gather the nations.

A flood – like a tidal wave watched over the world – a wave of destruction, anger, fear – the persecution – and few were left standing because of fear of life rather than love of God. The persecution did not stop and man became like animals

— their hearts darkened.

Then I saw the Bride and Groom appear, and the gathered nations proclaimed to the world the truth. Soon after, the gathered left the world that was destroyed, and the Bride, like a nurturing mother, nursed the wounds and brought living light to the earth.

But then I saw what the Bride saw as it left — and it went into descension before it ascended, it saw and experienced what I had only glimpsed. What I had thought was hell of the *Long Tzaddik* was nothing — because the Bride went into hell and knew the profoundness of wickedness until the Bride knew no kindness for wickedness, no mercifulness for the wickedness. The Bride felt it all and came out of it, for less than one day they had to taste of the punishment, just as the *Tzaddik* had to taste and be purified by learning. They were there — not only in spirit — soul — but in body. They saw it and felt it and smelled it and tasted it. And there in that they were protected. It was not simply watching the horrors of what was happening on the earth — they knew it as it was occurring above and below.

And then they rose up and were blessed and waited to return. Then I was heavy with the burden of the Bride, and I was heavy with the burden of those called to remain; and saw how they arced with one another. Like two halves of the feminine … one above … one below and between them — as in their safe keeping were the gathered believers.

I came back and I thanked God for showing me this vision.

I realized that as I go through the trials that are coming, none of us are alone. The days are shortened, because the Bride above bears in less than a day much of the horror, and those below bear in years so that many would be saved. And I saw how both – those above and below are sheltered and protected and guided through it all."

*****

The fourth chapter of the Third Book of Enoch tells us that Enoch was removed from the people-group of the Flood *"to be a witness against them in the high heavens to all the inhabitants of the earth, so that they wouldn't say, 'The Merciful One is cruel.'"* Have you ever thought about what it must have been like to be alive before the Flood? Intense!!!

"36 But concerning that day and that hour, no man knows, not even the angels in heaven, but the Father alone. 37 Just as in the days of Noah, so will be the coming of the Son of Man. 38 For as the people before the Flood were eating and drinking, marrying and giving in marriage, until the day Noah entered into the ark, 39 And they knew nothing until the Flood came and carried them all away; such will be the coming of the Son of Man. 40 Then two men will be in the field; one will be taken away and the other left. 41 Two woman will be grinding at the hand mill; one will be taken and the other left" (Matthew 24:37-41 Aramaic).

But it was not as intense as it will be in our day: *"21 For then there will be great suffering such as has never happened from the beginning of the world until now, and never will be again. ²²And if those days were not shortened, no flesh would live; but for the sake of the chosen ones those days will be shortened"* (Matthew 24:21-22 Aramaic).

Many believe that the extinction of the dinosaurs and the Flood was a result of Nibiru (Death Star) coming too close to the earth. Is it a coincidence that this every 3600 year phenom (+- 100 years) is on our radar today, as it was in the days of Noah?

[Please don't get in fear, because all things work for the good for those that love God and are called according to His purposes (Romans 8.28). This will be and is the greatest day for the sons of the Living God – the day of the "greater works" (John 14.12). So much fun in a way!!!]

[Think of Nibiru when you hear about the Destroyer, the Doomsday Planet, Plant X, Nemesis, Xena, Hercolubus, Ninth Planet, Tenth Planet, etc...]

Did you know that many scientists, Bible scholars and World Elitists believe that Nibiru is on its way right now?

We are going to look at the possibility of the Nibiru (Planet X) Phenom happening in our day, especially since the 144,000 Firstfruits are somewhat following in Enoch's pattern. Are the 144,000 Firstfruits being removed as a witness to this generation as well as bringing them hope?

When this Doomsday Planet comes through our solar

system every 3600 years, it causes severe havoc and switches the earth's magnetic poles.

The center of the Nibiru System is a dwarf star that's a binary star to our own sun. The two revolve around each other. It's just that Nibiru has a massive somewhat erratic elliptical orbit.

The Nibiru System consists of a dark star that's smaller than our sun with 7 orbiting bodies (planets some smaller than our moon and a couple larger than our earth). The **Dark Star** is called **NEMESIS** or **PLANT X**. The blue planet is the **Blue Pachina** in history and the planet larger than the earth is called **Nibiru**… also known as the planet of the crossing or the Destroyer.

The Bible refers to the Nibiru System as WORMWOOD in Revelation 8.11.

And also the "red dragon" in Revelation 12.3.

The tenth planet that we're concerned about is Wormwood, as it is called in the Bible. The Vatican refers to Nibiru as "Wormwood. [The Vatican has its own infrared telescope (Graham Observatory) in Arizona. David Meade speaks about: Father Malachi (professor of paleontology) knew about an inbound planet that would cause destruction of millions of people. Father Malachi indicated that it would appear between 2015 and 2025. The exact date is secret hidden in the archives of the Vatican. I believe it's called the Third Secret of Fatima.]

"10And the third angel sounded, and there fell a great star from heaven, burning as it were a lamp [another sun?]*, and it fell upon the third part of the rivers, and upon the fountains of waters; 11 And the name of the star is called Wormwood: and the third part of the waters became wormwood; and many men died of the waters, because they were made bitter" (Revelation 8:10-11 KJV).*

According to David Meade, world-renown Bible Scholar of Torah Codes Rabbi Matityahu Glazerson recently found evidence of a catastrophic strike by Nibiru (Planet X System) in the Jewish year 5777. It's Gregorian calendar equivalent is October 2016 – October 2017. He also found evidence in a Bible Matrix that the end of days may begin as soon as Hanukkah of 2016.

NASA announced finding the 10th planet on July 29, 2005 and they called it "Xena." Retired military man John Moore has some excellent YouTube videos on the subject as well as *Skywatch Media News*:

- "Preparing for Pole Shift. *Poss in 2017* John Moore - 2008 Speech" => https://www.youtube.com/watch?v=t5P8uDYrZ0Q

- John Moore "Top Special Forces Soldier Says Planet X Coming" => https://www.youtube.com/watch?v=e42_W21ZEQs

- Final Alert!! DECEMBER 2016 it is expected NIBIRU PLANET-X to move the axis of Earth (Please share) => https://www.youtube.com/watch?v=Fqz8JF0iogw

- NASA INSIDER PLANET X IS VERY CLOSE ! PREPARE FOR => https://www.youtube.com/watch?v=udB0MYwF3lI &t=1s

- Latest Planet X Nibiru The 2017 Arrival of Wormwood => https://www.youtube.com/watch?v=RlUr7ZBNLK Q

Deep underground military bases have dramatically increased since the 1980s. Military trying to protect their own from coronal mass injections from the sun, asteroid impacts, catastrophic flooding… CIA domestic relocating to Denver and NSA relocating to Utah. There's a massive underground city under DIA that can house 10,000 people. Trillions of dollars are being used to protect the elite, but we have the best protection of all – the Lord our God. Be wise and do what He tells you to do.

Last year, both the Pope and the Queen of England said 2015 may be our last Christmas. "Pope Francis is saying that this Christmas may be the last for humanity while the Queen of England has expressed: "Dark fears. This will be the last Christmas on earth." So what do these two major worldwide figures know that we don't?" The Queen visited the *NASA Goddard Space Flight Institute* last Spring having a "sudden" interest in science.

Nibiru's stats:

- Nibiru comes into our solar system every 3600 years, give or take 100 years.

- Astronomers have been watching Nibiru since the 1950s. [Source: NASA Insider]

- In 2008, Nibiru could be seen in high detail with infrared telescopes.

- Nibiru is a dwarf star that's a binary star to our own sun. The vast majority of solar systems are binary systems with two suns. This newly discovered brown dwarf is directly below our celestial south pole. We need to consider that our sun may have a sibling.

- Technically, our solar system has nine planets and a big sun. Nibiru has seven planets and its own sun. Nibiru is its own solar system. We are about to have a solar system come through the middle of our solar system. That can't be good. [Source: NASA Insider]

- Nibiru is 4-5 times (or 10 times) the size of the earth.

- Nibiru has 3-5 times the mass of Jupiter.

- Nibiru is a giant iron planet that they say is 47,000 miles across (diameter). It's composition is cesium, iron oxide, iron, oxygen and ozone. It looks just like our own sun, but it's a miniature sun giving off iron oxide dust around it. [Source: NASA Insider]

- Nibiru has an enormous dust cloud that goes all around it that is 50,000 – 100,000 miles on each side of it. [Source: NASA Insider]

- Nibiru's orbit compared to one year of earth's orbit is 10,000 – 20,000 years.

- Nibiru has been estimated to be traveling at 3500 mph. It has been picking up speed coming around the back side of the sun. It needs twice the speed coming around the back side of the sun. It needs twice the speed in order to attain breakaway speed to head back out in space. [Source: NASA Insider]

- Nibiru will appear as a second sun some months before the pole shift.

- Nibiru will probably be 20 million miles away when it crosses in front of us. Then as soon as Nibiru flips us upside down, we go into its debris field. [Source: NASA Insider]

- We won't technically see Nibiru in the sky until it is on us. [Source: NASA Insider]

- "When Nibiru goes by the earth, it is going to grab

our southern pole with its north pole. Then," the NASA Insider said, "It's gonna be like someone kicked this planet in the ass."

- There's going to be a massive earthquake when Nibiru locks unto us. [Source: NASA Insider]

- As Nibiru goes past us, we are going to follow it right upside down. Oceans will be roaring from pole-to-pole. Take a planet 7000 miles across and roll it upside down in 30 minutes, and you will have serious problems with wind and water. [Source: NASA Insider]

- You do not want to be on any coast or below 100 feet elevation.

Pole Shift stats:

- There has been 184 polarity changes of our earth according to Linda Moulton.

- The Director of the CIA (DCIA) says that the actual Pole Shift will probably happen from start to finish around 28 minutes. A NASA Insider says: "When you see it out there in the sky, run as fast as you can to an underground facility. It will happen very fast."

- The Pole Shift will cause 200 mph winds, massive tidal waves and earthquakes.

Remember in my friend's vision an earthquake proceeds God taking up the 144,000 Virgin Bride, like He did Enoch. Enoch is the witness in the high heavens to the people of the Flood that the Merciful One is not cruel. **I believe that the 144,000 Firstfruits will be the same in this Kingdom Day. They will testify that the Merciful One is not cruel. The 144,000 will also give faithful ones hope, because they are simply the first fruits of those being transfigured and they will be assisting those who remain on earth so many will be saved.**

How exactly are is Nibiru, the Pole Shift and earthquakes related to the 144,000? - It's a mystery – The 144,000 don't know exactly when they will be taken up by God (have a hunch that only the Father knows). The 144,000 have been told that they will be taken up soon and given time to prepare (tell families), just like Enoch.

In the *Ascension Manual*, MM Group Ascension #8 is shared. It is called the "Honeycomb Transformation and Synchronized Bridal Scrolls." In it, we experienced the Holy Spirit having a woven basket (symbolic of Christ and His Bride interwoven) with scrolls of humility and first fruits in it.

"You shall take of the first of all the fruit of the earth... and shall put it in a BASKET, and shall go unto the place which the LORD thy God shall choose to place His Name there" (Deuteronomy 26.2).

<u>Bikkurim</u> is The Feast of First Fruits. Bikkurim was the day

when Noah came out of the waters of death and rested on Mount Ararat. On the day of First Fruits, the Jews passed through the Red Sea to come up safely on the other side. On the day of First Fruits, the Jews were saved from certain death in Persia, and Haman was hung on his own gallows. On the day of First Fruit, Jesus was resurrected conquering death forever!

When the 144,000 Transfiguration takes place and people start getting transfigured, that's going to be the Greatest Show on Earth!!!

ENOCH's name is the noun form of the verb *hanok*, which is most commonly rendered "to offer," and "dedicated one." His father Jared named his son "dedicated (offered)" out of a desire to fully dedicate his son to God as the FIRST FRUIT of his godly life. The root of Enoch's name means "to inspire" or "to teach." There is only one record in the canon of Scripture of Enoch's deeds: "*14And Enoch also, the seventh from Adam, prophesied of these, saying, Behold, the Lord comes with ten thousand of His saints, 15to execute judgment upon all, and to convince all that are ungodly among them of all their ungodly deeds which they have ungodly committed, and of all their hard speeches, which ungodly sinners have spoken against Him: (Jude 1.14-15).* In the Books of Enoch there are many more.

What enabled Enoch to be ascend bodily and be transfigured is his walk with God. The Hebrew word for "walk" in Genesis 5.24 means "to subject oneself and follow." [Take note, because this applies to 144,000 and those who will follow them.] This walking with God is much more than traveling. It refers to taking each step in accordance with His will without having different thoughts. Ultimately, walking with God is to become one with God, so that the two may appear as one. This same Hebrew word for "walk" - *halak* – is used in Deuteronomy 30.16 and is associated with life: *" ¹⁵ See, I have set before thee this day life and good, and death and evil; ¹⁶ See, I have set before thee this day to love the LORD your God, to WALK in His ways, and to keep His commandments, and His statutes, and His judgments, that thou may live and multiply: and the LORD thy God shall bless thee in the land whither thou goes to possess it" (Deuteronomy 30.15-16).*

Enoch lived 308 years at the same time as Adam, and was snatched (taken) by God into heaven 57 years after Adam died. Adam spoke of the Garden of Eden and what it was like. Enoch's bodily ascension in order to be transfigured confirmed Adam's teachings and that the world of eternal life without death was not only real, but attainable.

The birth of Methuselah was a sign of the judgment of the Flood. Enoch fathered Methuselah at the age 65, and named his son "when he dies, judgment". Methuselah lived 969 years, which coincides precisely with the year of the flood:

Calculation:

Methuselah was 187 years old when he fathered Lamech;

Lamech was 182 years old when he fathered Noah;

The Flood occurred when Noah was 600 years old

$$187 + 182 + 600 = 969$$

The Flood happened 696 years after Enoch's Ascension and Transfiguration, because Enoch was taken by God when he was 365 years old.

*****

The leaves are blowing. The four winds and the angels are blowing the trumpets. The leaves that are blowing are the 144,000 people who make up the Virgin Bride. These are those who delight in God's Word and are like trees of righteousness planted by the river of the Water of Life, that brings forth fruit in season and his leaf doesn't wither. They are one glorious aspect of the leaves of the Tree of Life healing the nations (for the survival of humanity). The four winds and the angel blowing the Joel 2 trumpets are announcing the soon coming appearance of God's Metatron Merkabah Army.

"*¹And after these things, I saw four angels standing on the four corners of the earth, holding the four winds of the earth, that the wind should not blow on the earth nor on the sea nor on the tree. ² And I saw another angel and he ascended from the direction of the rising sun, having the seal of the living God; and he cried with a loud voice to the*

*four angels to whom it was given to hurt the earth and the sea, saying,
³ Do not hurt the earth, neither the sea nor the trees, till we have
sealed the servants of our God upon the brows. ⁴ And I heard the
number of those who were sealed; and it was a hundred and forty and
four thousand, of all the tribes of the children of Israel" (Revelation
7.1-4 Aramaic).*

*" ¹ Blessed is the man that walks not in the counsel of the ungodly,
nor stands in the way of sinners, nor sits in the seat of the scornful. ²
But his delight is the law of the LORD: and in His law does he
meditate day and night. ³And he shall be like a tree planted by the
rivers of water that brings forth his fruit in his season; his leaf also
shall not wither; and whatsoever he does shall prosper" (Psalms 1.1-3
KJV).*

*" ¹And he showed me a pure river of water of life, clear as crystal,
proceeding out of the throne of God and of the Lamb. ² In the midst of
the street of it, and on either side of the river, was there the Tree of
Life, which bare twelve manner of fruits, and yielded her fruit every
month: and the leaves of the tree were for the healing of the nations"
(Revelation 22,1-2 KJV).*

*" ¹ Blow ye the trumpet in Zion, and sound an alarm in my holy
mountain: let all the inhabitants of the land tremble: for the day of the
LORD comes, for it is nigh at hand; ²A day of darkness and of
gloominess, a day of clouds and of think darkness, as the morning*

spread upon the mountains: a great people and a strong; there has not been ever the like, neither shall be any more after it, even to the years of many generations. ³A fire devours before them; and behind them a flame burns: the land is as the garden of Eden before them, and behind them a desolate wilderness; yea, and nothing shall escape them. ⁴ The appearance of them is as the appearance of horses; and as horsemen, so shall they run. ⁵ Like the noise of chariots on the tops of mountains shall they leap, like the noise of a flame of fire that devours the stubble, as a strong people set in battle array [Metatron Merkabah Army]. *⁶ Before their faces the people shall be much pained: all faces shall gather blackness. ⁷ They shall run like mighty men; they shall climb the wall like men of war; and they shall march every one on his ways, and they shall not break their ranks: ⁸ Neither shall one thrust another; they shall walk every one in his path: and when they fall upon the sword, they shall not be wounded. ⁹ They shall run to and fro in the city; they shall run upon the wall, they shall climb up upon the houses; they shall enter in at the windows like a thief. ¹⁰ The earth shall quake before them; the heavens shall tremble: the sun and the moon shall be dark, and the stars shall withdraw their shining. ¹¹And the LORD shall utter His voice before His army: for His camp is very great: for He is strong that execute His word: for the day of the LORD is great and very terrible; and who can abide it?*

¹² Therefore also now, saith the LORD, turn ye even to Me with all your heart, and with fasting, and with weeping, and with mourning: ¹³And rend your heart, and not your garments, and turn unto the LORD your God: for he is gracious and merciful, slow to anger, and of great kindness, and repenteth him of the evil. ¹⁴ Who knows if He will return and repent, and leave a blessing behind him: even a meat offering and a drink offering unto the LORD your God?

15 Blow the trumpet in Zion, sanctify a fast, call a solemn assembly:
16 Gather the people, sanctify the congregation, assemble the elders.
Gather the children, and those that suck the breasts: let the
bridegroom go forth of his chamber, and the bride out of her closet. 17
Let the priests, the ministers of the LORD, weep between the porch
and the altar, and let them say, Spare thy people, O LORD, and
give not thine heritage to reproach, that the heathen should rule over
them: wherefore should they say among the people, Where is their
God? 18 Then will the LORD be jealous for his land, and pity his
people. 19 Yea, the LORD will answer and say unto His people,
Behold, I will send you corn, and wine, and oil, and ye shall be
satisfied therewith: and I will no more make you a reproach among the
heathen: 20 But I will remove far off from you the northern army, and
will drive him into a land barren and desolate, with his face toward
the east sea, and his hinder part toward the utmost sea, and his stink
shall come up, and his ill savor shall come up, because he hath done
great things.

21 Fear not, O land; be glad and rejoice: for the LORD will do great
things. 22 Be not afraid, ye beasts of the field: for the pastures of the
wilderness do spring, for the tree bears her fruit, the fig tree and the
vine do yield their strength. 23 Be glad then, ye children of Zion, and
rejoice in the LORD your God: for he has given you the former rain
moderately, and he will cause to come down for you the rain, the
former rain, and the latter rain in the first month. 24 And the floors
shall be full of wheat, and the vats shall overflow with wine and oil.
25 And I will restore to you, the years that the locust has eaten, the
cankerworm, and the caterpillar, and the palmerworm, my great army

which I sent among you. *²⁶And ye shall eat in plenty, and be satisfied and praise the name of the LORD your God, that has dealt wondrously with you: and my people shall never be ashamed. ²⁷And ye shall know that I am the LORD your God, and none else: and My people shall never be ashamed.*

²⁸And it shall come to pass afterward, that I will pour out My Spirit upon all flesh; and your sons and your daughters shall prophesy, your old men shall see visions: ²⁹And also upon the servants and upon the handmaidens in those days will I pour out My Spirit. ³⁰And I will show wonders in the heavens and in the earth, blood, and fire, and pillars of smoke. ³¹ The sun shall be turned into darkness, and the moon into blood, before the great and the terrible day of the LORD come. ³² And it shall come to pass, that whosoever shall call on the LORD shall be delivered: for in Mount Zion and Jerusalem hath said, and in the remnant whom the LORD shall call" (Joel 2:1-32 KJV).

ABOUT THE AUTHOR

Robin Main is a prophetic artist, author, speaker and teacher who equips people to be the unique and beautiful creation that they have been created to be. She flows in love, revelation and wisdom with her SPECIALTY being kingdom enlightenment.

Her MISSION is to enlighten the nations by venturing to educate and restore the sons of the Living God.

Her CALL is a clarion one to mature sons and the pure and spotless Bride who will indeed be without spot or wrinkle.

Her ULTIMATE DESIRE is that everyone be rooted and grounded in love, so they can truly know the height, width, breadth and width of the Father's love.

68384777R00109

Made in the USA
Lexington, KY
09 October 2017